COTTAGE MODELLING
for PENDON

CHRIS PILTON

FOR ROYE

The old 'Calley Arms', Wanborough. In the late 1920s Roye saw the thatch torn from this charming building and replaced with pink asbestos tiles. To his horror, further modernisation was also carried out in an equally unsympathetic way. He was so distressed at this crime that he felt compelled to record its former charm and decided to try to recapture its appearance and character in model form. The model he produced in the 1930s was the foundation upon which Pendon has slowly grown ever since.

Pendon Museum

ACKNOWLEDGEMENTS

My inspiration to model came from Roye England and the Pendon team who drew my attention to the beauty of the Vale of White Horse with their ambition to preserve something of the inter-wars scene in model form. The modelling methods I describe are almost entirely those developed by Roye — from the kind of card used to the delicate weathering technique.

My now greater awareness of buildings and countryside, the models I have made, and this book, would not exist but for Roye, and I owe him a great deal.

The book itself owes a lot to my father, and to Paul Karau and June Judge of Wild Swan Publications, who all gave much support and advice throughout the project. I much appreciate their patience. My photographs of the models would not have been possible without encouragement and instruction from Tony Smith, a leading light at Pendon and not unknown to Wild Swan.

For the correct terminology in the timber-framed buildings section, I must thank Richard Harris and his book *Discovering Timber-Framed Buildings* (Shire Publications).

Roye England, founder of Pendon Museum.

All photos taken by the author unless otherwise credited.
Cover and title page photos by A. E. Smith

Designed by Paul Karau
Printed by Netherwood Dalton Ltd., Huddersfield

Published by
WILD SWAN PUBLICATIONS LTD.
1-3 Hagbourne Road, Didcot, Oxon OX11 8DP

The typewriter intrudes on the author's retreat where cottage modelling normally takes place.

INTRODUCTION

The very fact that you are reading this introduction suggests that you are interested in vernacular architecture and modelling, a compatible combination of two fascinating subjects. The title of this book, *Cottage Modelling for Pendon*, may pose the question 'Who or what is Pendon?'. Pendon Museum of Landscape and Transport in Miniature is the focus of a group of people dedicated to presenting views of the past in model form. These views are displayed in a purpose-built structure in the village of Long Wittenham, near Abingdon, Oxfordshire (see inside rear cover for details of opening times).

The main exhibit at the Museum was conceived in the early 1930s by Roye England, a young Australian who has since settled in this country. It was to be representative of an area between Didcot and Swindon, The Vale of White Horse, and set in the period when he first discovered it around 1930. Apart from the landscape in general, a characteristic village was to be modelled and the 'Vale Scene', as it has become known, has been growing slowly for many years. The prototype buildings chosen for the scene have been selected for a variety of reasons, representing homes, trade establishments, farms, etc, sometimes purely for their attractive appearance. Prototypes have also been chosen to show the varied methods of construction and subsequent alteration seen in buildings of 'the Vale', spanning the times from the Elizabethan timber-framed buildings right up to our 1930s period, with council houses partly built with breeze blocks. Although Roye initially experimented with 1mm and 3.5mm scales, the models are constructed to the scale of 4mm to 1 foot and as far as I know, there have been no potential Pendon prototypes ruled out for what might have appeared to be an almost impossible feature to represent in model form. The problem of finding suitable materials and techniques simply have to be resolved. I have made a small contribution to Pendon's growth by modelling some of the cottages and how I have made them forms the subject of this book.

The sequence of the book largely follows the order in which I tackle each project, from the initial study stage to the final weathering, taking in descriptions of the time-consuming and patience-testing jobs that are associated with modelling 'the Pendon way': painting individual bricks, sticking on little strips of paper tiles, etc. I am aware that the very thought of painting individual bricks of 1mm high and 3mm long may be offputting to many people, but if you are not over-ambitious in trying to model a whole village to this standard but concentrate your efforts on one building at a time, you may be surprised to find that a 'Pendon style' cottage is possible within a reasonable time and perhaps agree that the effort can be very rewarding. A 'three up three down' thatched cottage could take me in the region of 200 hours to model satisfactorily, a long time I know, but then I only work at a steady pace and try to incorporate as much detail as I can. Some readers may choose to adopt only certain aspects of this work and save time by ignoring interiors, for instance, but I expect many people put in such hours creating models of aeroplanes, ships, railway locomotives, etc, so why not cottages? Surely they are not less deserving subjects. Representing the multiplicity of textures and materials found in cottages of all sizes, is to me very rewarding. The obvious pleasure shown by the owners of the prototypes I have modelled on seeing their cottage in miniature is also very gratifying.

So I hope those who wish to make models of real cottages find my notes useful and benefit from my experience and mistakes. Those who are simply curious as to how Pendon cottages are made, may never try it themselves, but some of the techniques may still be of interest.

As far as I am concerned, studying the many aspects and features of even the humblest cottage or outbuilding has increased my awareness and appreciation of my surroundings, and attempting to capture the spirit of a building in model form has proved a most satisfying way of enjoying each subject.

CHRIS PILTON 1987

This 1930s picture has the sort of atmosphere we at Pendon are trying to produce in our Vale scene: the warm summer's day feeling, and the way the road, cottage and trees are all in sympathy with one another.
Roye England

Recording dimensions, sketching and taking photographs to work from is often very pleasant, especially in a setting like this — a beautiful spot in Bishopstone.
Roye England

FIELDWORK & SCALE DRAWINGS

One of the buildings I have chosen as an example for this chapter is Wharf Cottage, Uffington, not an obviously attractive chocolate box sort of cottage but an interesting one full of character with an interesting pedigree. Built at what was once Uffington's own inland port, a basin on the Wilts & Berks Canal, this is a fascinating building with floors at differing levels through the various lean-tos and other extensions that make up the whole cottage.

The other building I have chosen to illustrate some of our recording methods is a small thatched cottage in Uffington called 'Styles' — a simple little dwelling of chalkstone (clunch) and brick with a half-hipped thatch – quite common construction for the Vale.

Having the delighted approval of the owners, photographs were taken of each aspect of the building, from far enough away to fit a complete elevation into the frame. After these general views, a series of close-ups were taken one after another along each wall, for greater detail. The roof received some individual attention as well, not forgetting detail shots of the two chimneys. These detail shots often prove invaluable, for although one intends to measure and take notes of everything that appears relevant, things can and do go wrong. For instance the tall chimney at the rear could not be reached for measuring, so the photographs were used to scale its height.

Just as we were counting bricks, the good lady of the house invited us in for coffee, generously laced with whisky (we were in the depths of winter). Some time later we emerged from the snug little cottage to pick up where we had left off. However, the chimney was forgotten until we were looking at the field notes back at home, many miles from Styles Cottage. Thank goodness for those detail photos!

I am not experienced to comment on the technicalities of photography, but really expensive equipment is not essential. For our purposes some reasonably acceptable photographs can be obtained using a humble Instamatic camera. Both black and white and colour prints have their good and bad points, but as long as they are accompanied by notes of the colours and tones, either will do. For example, brickwork in one area of a building could be an orange-red and in another area a brown sort of red, the lichens on roofs could be of the golden yellow or greenish-whitish-greyish types. Sometimes, especially on a derelict building, it is possible to chip off samples of brick, slate etc. to remind you of the colours, but these can only be a guide as apart from the difficulties of a scaled down impression, the weathering on the sample may not be representative of the whole. I find slides inconvenient for both viewing and handling reasons.

The surveying of any building requires something to measure with and something on which to record the measurements. I use a 66 ft tape and make notes on sketched elevations of each aspect on A4 paper secured to a clip-board.

The measuring of Styles Cottage started by establishing that (luckily) the ground line appeared to be level, and so could correspond to the datum line of the model and have all the vertical measurements above it.

Plate 1. My father and myself outside Wharf Cottage in 1981. This view was taken looking south from the site of a former lifting bridge on the lost Wilts & Berks Canal, with Uffington church and the Berkshire Downs beyond. *Roye England*

Plate 2. Measuring and recording Styles Cottage. *Roye England*

Plate 3. The model of Wharf Cottage showing the extensive artificial card 'cellar' for handling purposes. This is later concealed in the surrounding landscape.

A. E. Smith

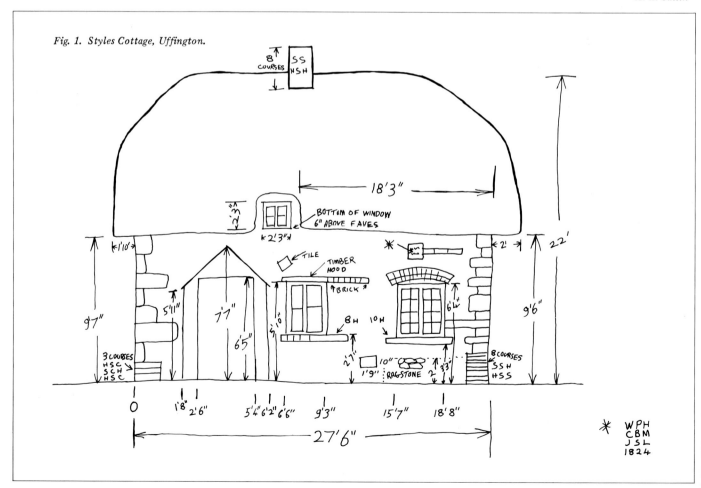

Fig. 1. Styles Cottage, Uffington.

On Wharf Cottage, Uffington, the ground line was anything but level, and Martin and Mary Heard, Pendon's official buildings recorders, had to establish a level line around the building. They chose the eaves level on the central rendered section. From this datum the verticals could be measured above and below where necessary, working around the cottage.

At Styles Cottage the starting position was the left-hand end of the front wall. My father and I measured the horizontals, all starting from zero, firstly to the left edge of the porch, then successively along the frontage, to places such as each side of the porch, door and windows, until the far end of the wall was reached, thus giving intermediate and overall distances, as in *Fig. 1*. Running dimensions are far more accurate than individual dimensions added together.

The projection of the porch was recorded on the end elevation sketches, as were the projections of the lean-to outbuildings at the rear. As these were additions built at right angles to the main structure, recording the distances was quite simple. With Wharf Cottage, on the other hand, there were angles other than 90°. These distances were determined by measuring offsets from a base line, as in *Fig. 2*.

The majority of vertical measurements on buildings of this type can be obtained with the aid of a step-ladder and/or a fishing rod or even a long cane with a nail in the end on which to hang the measuring tape. Putting its top to the required high position, a finger of the spare hand can be held at the bottom of the rod, from where a colleague should usually be able to measure to the ground or a window sill or anything that will serve as a datum. If used on its own, the length of the fishing rod will have to be known and included in the overall height. The height of the ridge on Styles Cottage was determined with the assistance of a large extendable aluminium ladder that had been left by a thatcher who had only just finished his work on the roof. If the ladder had not been available the height of the ridge could have been arrived at by offering the tape to the ridge on the end of a cane, or even on small buildings by laying the cane or fishing rod on the sloping roof to determine the distance from the eaves to the ridge. The distance from eaves to eaves across the end of the cottage can then be measured to complete the dimensions required for the construction of a triangle back at the drawing board, as shown in *Fig. 3*. Of course the height of buildings, chimneys, etc, can be arrived at by optical

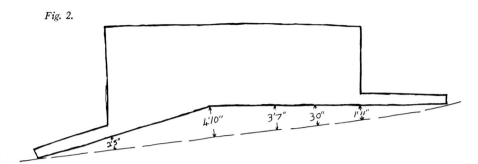

Fig. 2.

triangulation, but that's outside my experience.

The position of the chimney in the ridge had to be estimated by eyeing in the edge of it, vertically to a position on the wall that could be measured, as in *Fig. 4*.

SCALE DRAWINGS

With the field notes completed and the photographs printed, I start converting the information into 1:76 scale drawings, i.e.

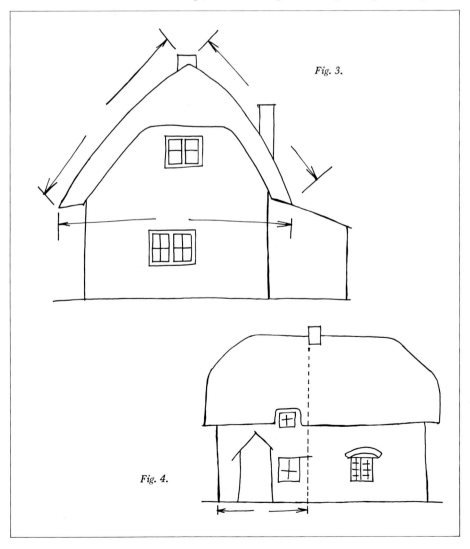

Fig. 3.

Fig. 4.

4 mm to 1 foot, preferably while the memory of the visit to the prototype is still fresh. A drawing board with sliding cursor (built-in tee-square) is not essential, but is of great assistance — likewise compasses, dividers and set-square. The layout of the drawings I make (as far as I know) does not conform to any architectural or engineering practice. If possible I like to have all elevations and the ground plan on one sheet of paper, usually starting with the ground plan. I try to be

as accurate as possible in preparing the drawings as many dimensions will simply be transferred directly to the card that will eventually become the model. For conversion of the prototype measurements on the field notes into 1:76 scale measurements I use a conversion table that I have prepared for myself. This is quite a time and brain-saving aid. On the other hand, 4 mm to one foot is simple enough to work with when every millimetre represents 3″ or every half millimetre 1½″ etc.

The buildings I have used to illustrate a simple ground plan are a thatched barn and adjoining stone-roofed stable. They stand in the village of Denchworth in the flat part of the Vale, and were modelled separately before being joined together (see *Plate 4*).

The ground plan for such simple buildings can be drawn with the tee-square or cursor and set-square, as all corners are right angles (see *Fig. 5*).

A more complex ground plan is illustrated by Mill Cottage, Woolstone — possibly not calendar material, but almost. I seem to remember Howard Fuller, Pendon's secretary and ground scenery chief, describing it as a sort of Hansel and Gretel ginger-bread house, nestling in its trees as it does. Actually it is another conglomoration of styles and materials of different periods so often found in country cottages (see *Plate 5*).

Plate 4. Barn and stable from Denchworth.   *A. E. Smith*

Fig. 5.

| box no. 1 | box no. 2 |

The plan of the main building (Fig. 6) is straightforward enough, but the complex of small outhouses is less so. The task of drawing a plan to work from was made quite easy for me as Martin and Mary Heard had done an excellent job of measuring at the site. The yard was in effect triangulated by measuring radially from the corner of the house out to the beginning and end of each little outbuilding, having already determined the frontage of each. I copied this technique for the production of the scale drawing and was satisfied than no errors had crept in.

The Denchworth Farm buildings (Fig. 7) provide a simple example of the sort of scale elevations from which I work — not much undulation in the ground line and no particularly significant stones worth drawing.

The stone and brick stable section consists of nearly all straight lines which posed no problems in drawing. The arches over the door and windows were also no problem once the correct radius had been established — very often with the point of the compasses somewhere down at ground level. The sagging ridge, curving eaves and bulging walls of the barn were drawn freehand, joining up known points along the building.

Plate 5. Mill Cottage, Woolstone.

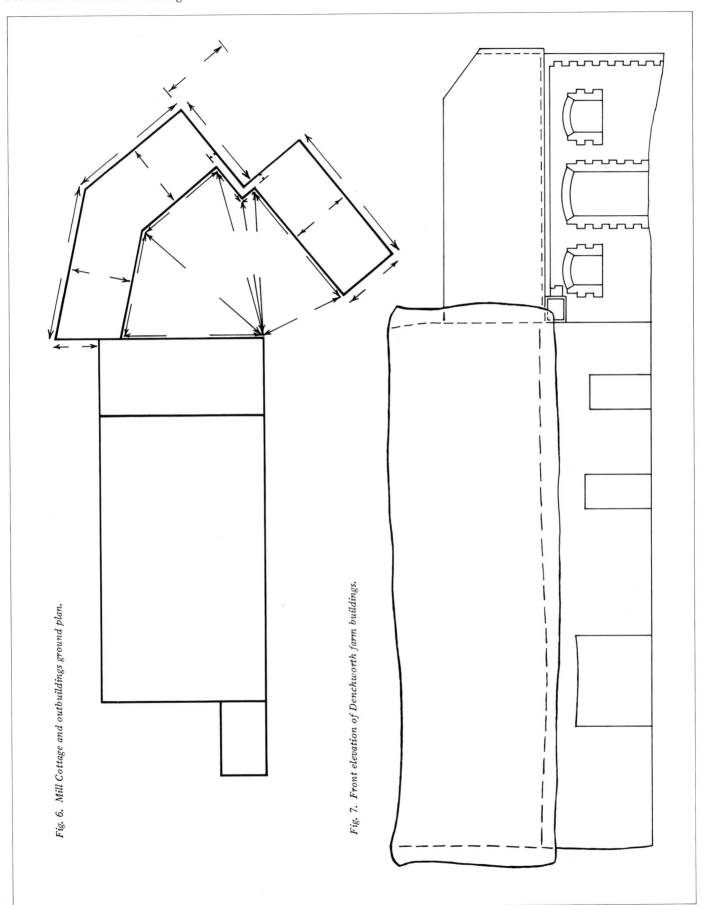

Fig. 6. *Mill Cottage and outbuildings ground plan.*

Fig. 7. *Front elevation of Denchworth farm buildings.*

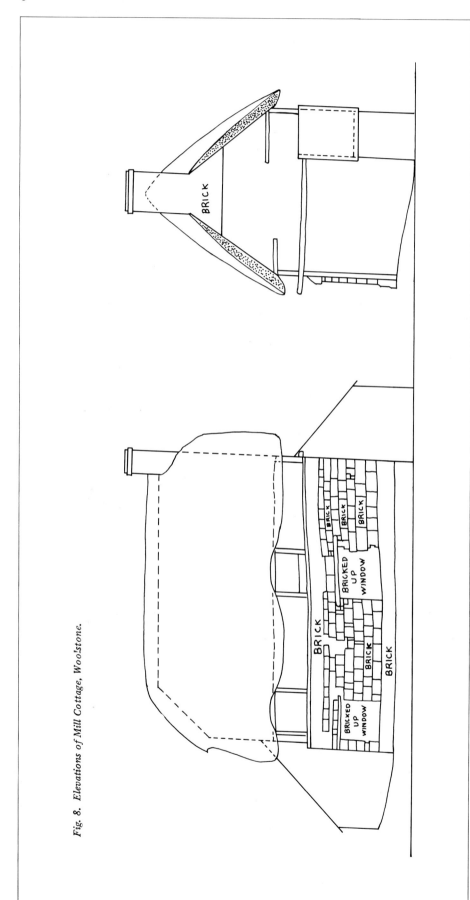

Fig. 8. Elevations of Mill Cottage, Woolstone.

The next illustration (Fig. 8) shows the east end and rear elevations of Mill Cottage. The whole house had settled and was leaning both to the east and north by some 6 inches at the eaves. So, although the corners were reasonably straight, they were not upright. This effect is very easy to represent at the drawing stage as the tops of corners should therefore be 2mm out of vertical from their bottoms. With these lines drawn, the walls assume their correct shape almost a parallelogram, as in *Fig. 8*.

On the rear elevations of Mill Cottage the stones are identified as well as the brickwork — unlike the Denchworth stable. The reason for this was that the chalkstone blocks were large enough and made a pattern worth laying out on the drawing rather than just copying on to the card from the field notes and photographs. The rising ground line was drawn by following the lie of the land recorded on the field notes, from the imaginary datum. I seldom include much detail in the windows as the final positions of glazing bars, for instance, are adjusted on the model when they are being glued in place. Also I usually only represent roofs and chimneys as outlines, although I sometimes partially represent either slates, tiles or thatch.

I find this amount of drawing sufficient to check whether my measurements of the prototype will in fact combine to produce a satisfactory model. Some Pendon modellers have a lot more faith in the field notes and consider the making of scale drawings unnecessary. My attitude is that I would much rather discover an error of measurement on an expendable drawing than on the card which in due course will become the model. The scale drawings are not necessarily any improvement on the field notes and photographs but, having made them, I am reassured that an error in the initial measuring will not be reproduced in the model. I still get such details as brick bonds and some stonework bonds from the field notes and photographs. I like to have the photographs sorted into collections of one elevation, as I often only work on one elevation at a time. If I have a particular detail to check on, the already sorted photographs reduce the searching time considerably.

So, it's either a lot of faith in your field notes and your eventual interpretation, or a little less, backed with scale drawings. Whether or not you choose the latter I strongly recommend a drawing board with sliding cursor for it is most useful during the next stages, laying out the card, embossing and painting.

ESSENTIAL CONSIDERATIONS

Plate 6. A sleepy country pub with a warm straw hat, 'The Leather Bottle', just near the Great Western main line running through the Vale of White Horse at Challow. This pub is now much altered compared with this 1950s photograph.   *Miss Comley*

THE CARD

The Pendon method of making folds (where possible) at the corners instead of joins, means that not just any old card is appropriate. The material which I use for making Pendon buildings was bought in Bristol in 1941 by Pendon's founder, Roye England, just before the shop was destroyed by enemy bombing. He bought £10 worth, which in those days meant a good large stock that has lasted well ever since. Although bought in Bristol, the card was not in fact Bristol Board (apparently its skin is too brittle). It was apparently called 'International Pasteboard' and came in sheets varying in thickness from 0.2 mm to 0.75 mm.

Unfortunately, this legendary material is no longer available and I have not found an exact substitute. However, Apsley White Pasteboard comes very close in quality, with regard to colour acceptance and embossing retention, and shows no greater tendency towards splitting at folded corners. At the time of writing it can be obtained in various thicknesses, ranging from: 0.3 mm (12 thou.) to 1.25 mm (50 thou.).

I acquired my stock from the manufacturer, Dickenson Robinson, Apsley Mills, Herts, but try your local printer or art shop.

Plate 7. A gorgeous scene in front of 'The Leather Bottle', captured in the early 1950s. The fair-haired lady is Miss Comley who took over the running of the pub from her father, just before the Second World War. The inviting 'come on in for a drink' feeling I get from this photo is the sort of atmosphere I strive to reproduce so that one can almost smell the scent of the malted barley and hops coming from the open door and windows. With a two-dimensional photo or painting one can only imagine what is inside or around the corner, but with a model one can move around it and have a look.   *Miss Comley*

Plate 8. The Leather Bottle Inn, Challow.
A. E. Smith

The card is white, but one side can have an almost undetectable regular pattern (impressed into its surface) that unfortunately becomes more obvious when painted. If a bench lamp is adjusted to shine across the surfaces of the card, the one to avoid should become apparent. The skin of this card is made up of several layers that can be peeled off to represent flaked away plaster etc. The outer layer is quite strong, yet soft and pliable, a quality required for embossing and corner folding.

For walls, I have used the 0.55 mm thickness material (550 microns, just over ½ mm) and by taking the usual precautions (as mentioned later) the card has behaved very well, although its effective lifetime has not been tested in the way the card Roye bought in 1941 has.

Not all Pendon 'cottage models' have been made with pasteboard; Penny Thompson, who has made a good number of Pendon buildings, used a thicker card known as 'Ticket Board' which may be more readily available. Whatever is used, it should have a matt white, or near white, surface, be sufficiently stable to give one enough confidence to get it quite wet without ruining its composition, have a soft strong skin capable of the delicate folding described later, and accept water colour readily, without being too absorbent.

CELLARS

As can be seen in *Plate 8*, the bottom of the wall card is actually some 30 mm below the ground line. This is the only area of the model that can be held, and it is apparent in many of the photographs that this area can get quite grubby. Obviously one would not want this to happen to the paintwork which is very easily smudged with the least sweaty fingers. Even with meticulously clean hands, a 'cellar' as we

call it, is essential. Another reason for the 'cellar' is that in many cases the ground line is anything but level, see for example, Wharf Cottage in *Plate 3*.

Flat baseboards with level ground scenery and buildings such as this simply do not go together. At Pendon the ground scenery

undulates considerably in places, and buildings have been positioned so that the ground lines of the prototype are reproduced and incorporated in our own contours. With the 'cellars' set in the ground, structures appear to grow out of the scenery instead of sitting on top of it.

Plate 9. Breakspeare's Cottage, Knighton. I have a particular soft spot for this model as it was my first cottage. Another reason may be the 'cat slide' on the left nearly reaching from ridge to ground level.   *A. E. Smith*

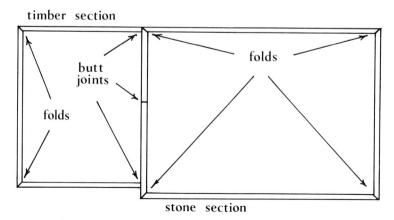

Fig. 9. 'Kit arrangement' plan of Breakspeare's Cottage.

KIT ARRANGEMENTS

Before any card is cut, the positions of the folds and joins have to be decided upon. With a simple little cottage such as Breakspeare's Cottage, Knighton, the procedure was fairly obvious: a four-sided box folded at the corners for the main stone-built portion, and a three sided box for the timber section. A butt joint was made in the end of the main box that would be hidden by the timber section as in *Fig. 9*.

At the place where the two boxes would be joined there was a step in the front wall; this feature, coupled with the change in building materials, decided the issue.

Wharf Cottage was a little more complicated; again there were changes of building materials at points where extensions had been added. At many of these places there was no evidence of the walls being bonded together and so a conveniently straight line existed between two types of stone or between brick-work and stonework (see *Plate 10*).

Some of the reasons why exposed joints are felt to be undesirable, and another 'kit arrangement' for a prototype made up of successive additions, can be found on page 76 where the modelling of The Old Vicarage at Steventon is described.

Plate 10. A view of the un-bonded changes in material at the rear of Wharf Cottage. At these places butt joints could be employed that would not need disguising extensively. The model of Wharf Cottage was made up of many separate sections, so the 'kit arrangement' for the model needed much thought before the final decisions were made (see *Fig. 10*). *A. E. Smith*

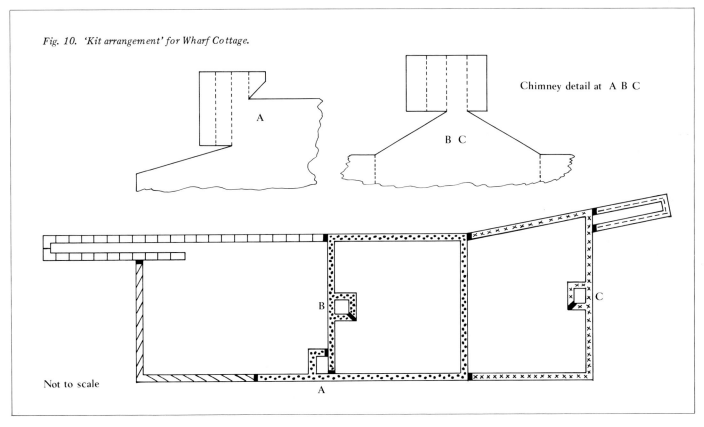

Fig. 10. 'Kit arrangement' for Wharf Cottage.

Chimney detail at A B C

Not to scale

Plate 11. Willis' Cottage as photographed in 1984. *Martin Heard*

LAYING OUT THE CARD

The usual thickness of card I use for walls is 0.6 mm which, when exposed at door and window apertures, represents a scale 2″. As the frame is usually set back in the reval, this thickness is acceptable in the majority of cases, but, if a door or windowframe is flush with the outside of the wall, the 2″ edge is used to represent the frame instead. This may be a little on the thin side for the exposed area of many door frames and possibly a little thick for many window frames, but in my experience the compromise is usually acceptable (see *Fig. 11*).

The example I have used for 'laying out the card' is Willis' Cottage, Steventon, a timber-framed and probably thatched cottage of the 17th century, considerably altered in the late 18th or early 19th centuries. The bay windows to the left of the front door date from 1939, after the period depicted at Pendon, so will not appear on the model.

Not being a particularly complex building, the 'kit arrangement' for Willis' Cottage was not a complicated one, though I have drawn it here with identification numbers at different positions around the ground plan. These will also appear on my drawing of the card in the early stages of being marked out.

An adequate piece of card is secured to the drawing board with masking tape, in a convenient position for the many different processes to be carried out. The first line drawn is a reference line, usually 30 mm (the depth of 'cellar') above the bottom of the card and running its full length. The positions of

Fig. 11.

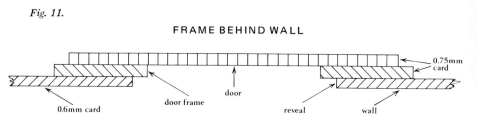

FRAME BEHIND WALL

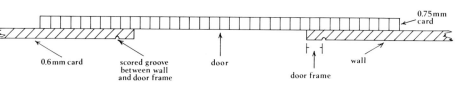

FLUSH FRAME

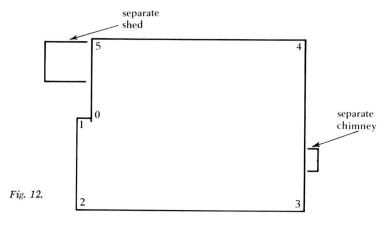

Fig. 12.

WILLIS' COTTAGE PLAN

Fig. 13. First stages of marking out Willis' Cottage.

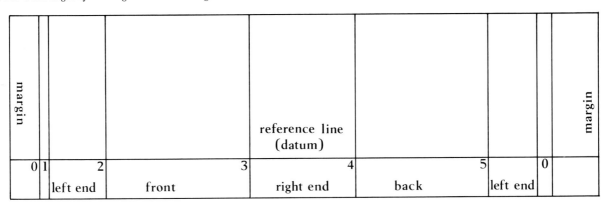

Fig. 14. Cutting lines marked for Willis' Cottage.

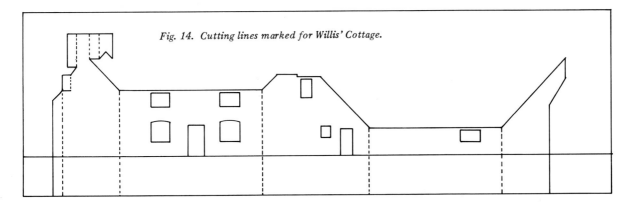

the corners that will later be folds are drawn faintly across the reference line. I keep the pencil lines marked on the surface to be painted as feint as possible, as darker ones may not later rub out very well, either leaving a mess or a depression in the card. I often use an ordinary HB pencil, as a feint line requires less pressure than say a 3H, although the HB may need sharpening more often.

On each corner line I then mark the tops of the walls and along the reference line only the positions of the doors and windows. As mentioned earlier, I usually use dividers to transfer measurements from the scale drawings to the card: when transferring successive dimensions along one line I always start at zero on both drawing and card. The marks I make are in fact small holes (virtually pin pricks) where I break the surface of the card with the dividers. When marking cutting positions for door and window apertures, it is worth double checking that the dots correspond with the edge to be cut.

Having established the horizontal distances, the verticals are lightly marked. With a set-square on the cursor and one end of the dividers placed into the appropriate hole in the reference line, the set-square is then brought along to meet the dividers; the dot

that will indicate either a top or bottom corner can now easily be made in the correct place against the set-square. The operation takes nowhere near as long as it takes to read my explanation. I hope those of you who are accustomed to this sort of work (or shudder at my primitive methods) will bear with me for the sake of those who are not. With the corner positions marked, I faintly draw in the eaves line and door and window outlines (see *Fig. 14*). The chimney on the left-hand end has been included because it is in the same vertical plane as the wall; the apparent wings on either side will be folded to make its other faces. The join will, of course, have to be a good one but has been planned to be out of sight given normal viewing conditions. My description of making chimneys can be found on page 40.

As can be seen in *Fig. 14* the front downstairs windows have arched soffits (tops). Often the crowns of such arches are approximately one course of bricks above the spring of the arch. The three positions A, B and C in *Fig. 15* need to be joined with an accurate arc, best drawn with compasses. There are technical ways of finding the true centre of the arc, but for downstairs windows I have found on many buildings that the radius can be

Fig. 15.

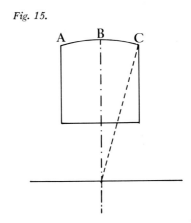

simply achieved with the compass point on the ground line or just below. The lines shown in *Fig. 14* are the ones to cut to, so they must be in the right places; anything not obvious must be clarified. If there is a door with a flush frame I often indicate this with a double line (see *Fig. 16*), the inside one being the one to cut to. When a window frame is flush with the wall, any intermediate upright, often with the same proportions as the outside members, may need to be catered for at this stage (unlike windows with a reveal when this centre upright is dealt with at a later stage).

So for the flush-framed window I draw a line which represents the joint between the wall and the frame, and inside this another line for the inside edge of the frame. The area within this line is then divided to give the necessary number of sections (glazed areas) between the intermediate uprights. The large sections will be cut out leaving any uprights flush with the rest of the frame and the wall.

Before going further I cut out the door and window apertures, particularly as stone and brickwork needs representing in the 'reveals' (not the 'flush frames'). I often leave the marked out card on the drawing board and slip a piece of inferior quality card underneath the area to be cut, thus preventing damage to the drawing board. The next step is to insert a new blade in the craft knife (new blades are cheap enough and the resulting cleaner cuts more than justify the expense, so buy a good stock!). I use the ordinary plastic handled 'Swan Morton' knife with No. 1 blades whereas others prefer a scalpel. I usually start with the vertical lines, placing the point of the knife at the top of the line, I then bring a 6″ steel rule up to it (checking of course that the rule is clean). With the rule parallel to the line, the knife is gently drawn along (at a shallow angle), not pressing too hard into the card or against the rule. Two or three strokes may be necessary to cut through — one heavy cut can produce poor edges. Considerable care is taken to avoid leaving little rags of card in the corners, this is done by not cutting along the full length of a line but by stopping short of the corner. I then turn the job around, drawing board and all, and start at the other end of the same line and cut into the middle, being careful to run exactly into the previous cut, otherwise a thin sliver of

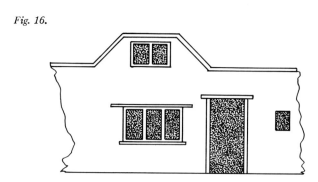

Fig. 16.

card is produced which projects from what ought to be a continuous straight line. Working along the card I cut all the vertical lines for three-quarters of their length, then all cuts are completed from their opposite ends. For the horizontals I turn the drawing board so that the lines to be cut run towards me and not from side to side. By gently pulling the knife toward myself, I find I have better control and thus a better chance of accuracy, but that's a personal preference. After cutting all four sides of a door, for instance, the scrap card may well have come out of the aperture without any assistance but, if not, I do not tear it out as the dreaded rags will surely appear at the corners. When the scrap piece does not come out easily some further cutting is required. Taking care that the blade is following the original cut exactly, this is best done, in my opinion, free-hand, for if the straight edge were used again, I fancy I would be concentrating on keeping the blade against it rather than in the original cut. In the case of a flush window frame, any centre or intermediate upright has to remain intact.

These will not become distorted in the cutting process if the two pieces of scrap card either side of it are left in place until both can be detached easily. If this is not done, what is shown in *Fig. 17* can often happen.

For curved soffits I still work from each end, closely following the arc. I prefer to cut free-hand but a coin will often coincide with the radius required and provide a cutting guide. It is best to get this sort of job right first time as trimming is not at all easy and very often will leave what should be a smooth arc in a series of stepped straight lines.

Fig. 17.

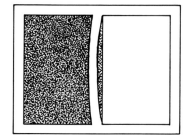

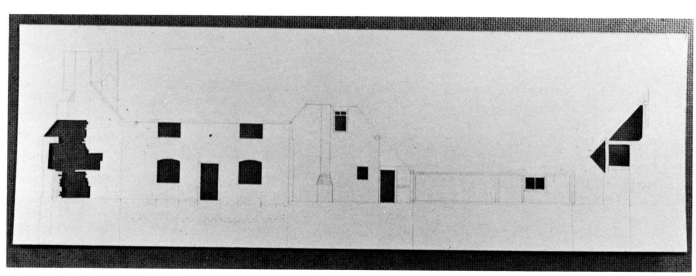

Plate 12. The beginnings of Willis' Cottage with the door and window apertures cut out. The other cut-out areas at each end are for special textures described on pages 88 and 89.

CREATING THE VISUAL EFFECT

Plates 13a and 13b. *Left:* The variety of bonds and brick colours found in many rural buildings are largely unnoticed but nevertheless have a real effect on their overall character. This is particularly so with panels of brick infill in timber-framed buildings. *Right:* A mixture of brick and plain daub panels within the frame of The Old Vicarage. *A. G. Pilton and Author*

BRICKWORK

The texture of brickwork walls (or more accurately the mortar courses between them), is represented by depressing the card into grooves to represent the mortar lines between courses, leaving individual bricks in relief. The surface of the card, when painted, is rough enough to represent the brick faces. The outlines of flush door and window frames, lintels and other such timbers, are also depressed to represent the mortar separating them from the brickwork. Before covering the tools and methods involved in embossing it is necessary to understand the way the bricks are laid or the pattern of 'bonding'.

BRICK WALLS

I have come across one prototype wall that was built with one brick placed directly upon another and so on up the wall as in *Fig. 18*, but this was merely decorative infill on a modern building. They have usually had some bond or other so that one join does not immediately correspond with another. Some understanding of the more common bonds is helpful when trying to copy from a particularly bad photograph or when conjecture is unavoidable.

Fig. 18.

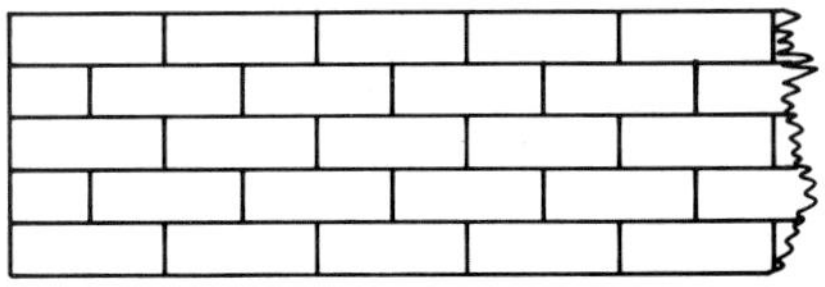

Fig. 19. Stretcher or running bond. This is very common in more recent 20th century buildings where a single outer skin (i.e. 4½" thick) encloses a cavity. However, panels of infill (again only 4½" thick) in timber-framed buildings are sometimes of this bond.

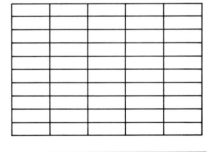

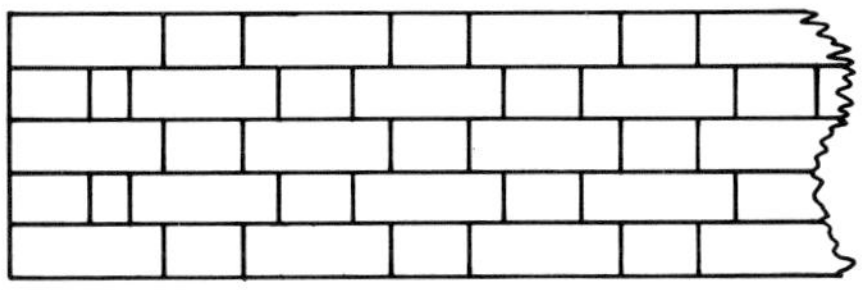

Fig. 20. Flemish bond. A non-cavity 9 inch thick wall often found in railway and industrial buildings as well as rural ones.

Fig. 21. Flemish garden wall bond. Not restricted to garden walls but used when both sides of the wall would be seen. In earlier years hand-made bricks varied in length. This bond was more economic of the headers (bricks laid across the wall) which had to be the same length.

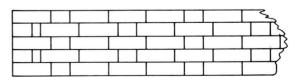

Plate 14. Flemish bond brickwork used in the building of the stable that accompanies The Leather Bottle Inn.

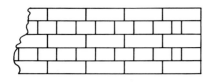

Fig. 22. English bond. Another non-cavity wall commonly used in railway buildings as well as other buildings in urban and rural areas.

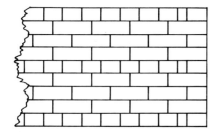

Fig. 23. English garden wall bond. Another bond not exclusive to garden walls but used when economy of headers and bricks in general was felt to be desirable.

Plate 15. Variation on Flemish garden wall bond used in the 'gents' at The Leather Bottle Inn.

PLAN

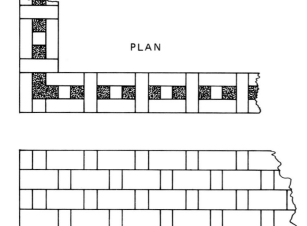

Fig. 24. Rat trap bond. Not a particularly common bond but a very economical one (using bricks on their side to gain height) with both headers and stretchers placed on edge to the Flemish pattern.

SIDE ELEVATION

Plate 16. Rear of Wharf Cottage, where the brickwork is in English garden wall bond.

Plate 16a. A rounded corner, made almost entirely of headers, except at the ends of the curve, where stretchers assist in bonding (to the stone portion and the straight brick wall that abuts the other building, which is the Friends Meeting House).

Fig. 25. Herring bone bonds. Various herring bone and similar decorative bonds can be found especially as filled panels in timber-framed buildings. Here are some I have seen.

Plate 17. Adjusted bond around a door and windows in The Leather Bottle Inn. The pale areas of brick are decorative patterns of pinkish grey headers.

Some walls are made almost entirely of headers, apart from stretchers and closers (half headers usually) around windows and at corners, and variations on the common bonds can also appear, so it is advisable to study the pictures and copy the prototype as much as possible. Closers are needed in many bonds and not only at corners. The area between upstairs and downstairs windows may continue uninterrupted for the length of the wall but the bond is often adjusted either side of the windows.

For many centuries buildings of all sorts have incorporated decorative patterns in the brickwork, often with bricks that have been fired in such a way as to alter their normal colour. In Flemish bond, for example, the headers in different walls can be either blue, a pinkish-grey, a mauveish-grey, a pale blueish-grey and sometimes a dull pale yellow. All these bricks can have an almost glazed finish, but can also have a granular and apparently burnt surface.

Decorations also come in the form of bricks projecting from the main wall by differing amounts. Courses of such bricks have names such as Dog Teeth and Dentils. Special bricks in fancy shapes can also appear in patterns or to enhance reveals etc. In modelling for Pendon I have not so far had to represent any of these features, so all I can suggest is that overlays of specially cut card or paper be attached to the model before painting; some may be best achieved by gluing on individual bricks. Chimneys with projecting string courses are covered on page 40.

Fig. 26.

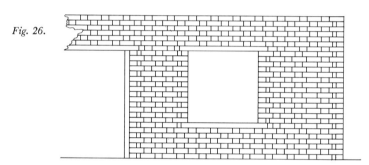

EMBOSSING THE CARD FOR BRICKWORK

The first step is to indicate the bond to be followed on the card; this I do with rows of dots or rather little holes made with a needle in a wooden handle. Two or more rows of dots are made beneath the ground line in the 'cellar' area and another row vertically in the margin at the end of the wall. The vertical dots (which correspond with the horizontal mortar lines) begin at the reference line and are spaced at approx 1 mm intervals. This depends on the building concerned for although most bricks are nominally 3 inches, it is rare to find that, for instance, twelve courses occupy a depth of only 36″. More likely you will find that only 11 or even 10 courses fit in the measured yard. This varies with bricks and the thickness of mortar. The answer, as always, is to study your chosen prototype. The horizontal rows beneath the reference line (which correspond with the ends of the bricks) may be separated to indicate the general alternating courses and the adjusted bond at either sides of doors and windows, as shown in *Fig. 26* and *Plate 18*.

Although such bond-adjusted areas will have been measured, errors do creep in, and for one reason or another they may turn out either too long or too short when marked on the card to incorporate the correct number of bricks. It is wise to check for this possibility before making the dots from which to work. If it does not work out exactly, then I start correctly at either end and work towards the middle, and make the unprototypical adjustment there; it is far more important to have the corners correct than the almost no-mans-land between. When working the bond around a corner, the bricks at what is the fold line have to be a brick and a half long, stretcher on one side of the line and header on the other side. When folded, this will suggest that we are viewing two sides of the same brick. The marking out of any separate chimneys to be added later is done in just the same way. An illustration of this can be found on page 40.

Having got the lines of dots marked, 1 mm apart for the courses and 3 mm per stretcher and 1½ mm per header, I then emboss the horizontal mortar lines. My 'horizontal brick embossing implement' is in fact a slightly blunt paper knife filed at the end so as to leave an impression in the card of under a ¼ mm wide, *without* breaking the surface. When making one of these or adapting any suitable implement, it is essential to be sure the results achieved with it are satisfactory, so try it out on scrap pieces of the same material before you risk spoiling the model. This tool is placed against the cursor in line with the highest dot in the vertical row, it is then drawn along with what I'm afraid I can only describe as the appropriate amount of pressure applied. I work from the top downwards so that I can see that the course heights are constant. Although the dots may be accurate it is very easy to produce varied course heights if one cannot see each preceding one properly. When embossing horizontally, care must be taken not to let the tool stray into areas such as the arches above doors and windows, door and window frames when flush, or lintels and other timbers.

Now we come to the vertical mortar lines. Some modellers use the same tool for horizontals and verticals, but my 'vertical brick embossing implement' is a modified watchmaker's screwdriver with which I depress the surface of the card; the blade is 1 mm wide and appropriately thin. The cursor is moved to just beneath the rows of dots in the cellar area, and a set-square is placed against the first dot in from the right. As I am right-handed I start at the right-hand end and work to my left so as not to cover what is being produced. With the tool against the square I depress the surface of the card between alternate courses. I must admit that when working my way up the wall I usually think to myself 'get one — miss one — get one — miss one' to ensure that only alternate courses are embossed from one dot. I usually complete the embossing from one row of dots before working from another, so the whole wall has alternate blank courses.

The blank courses are once again embossed starting from the right-hand end. If by following the dots the fresh courses do not fall in exactly the right place in relation to the courses already completed, the adjustment may perhaps best be done free-hand, placing the embossing tool in the correct position beneath the brick above and moving the square up to it to align the remainder. This adjustment does, of course, make some bricks a bit too short and others a bit too long. As I am usually concerned with old hand-made bricks, these variations in length are quite acceptable and may even be desirable. For

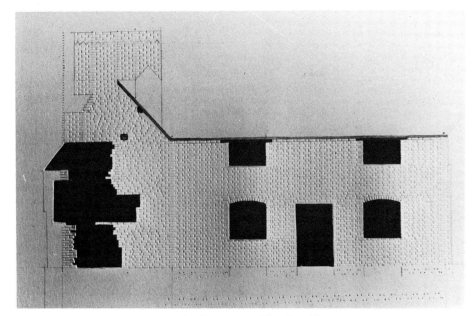

Plate 18. Rows of guiding dots indicating course and bond positions.

railway buildings though, a much more mechanical appearance is usually required and so great care must be taken to ensure the square does not wander. As with the horizontal mortar lines, I cannot measure or describe the amount of pressure applied to the vertical embossing tool. In my experience I have found that too much pressure will distort the card unacceptably and that insufficient pressure will cause the mortar lines to disappear when the mortar colour is applied. However, all these variables depend on the tool used and the material.

Usually the walls are embossed completely without the interruption of any other process; however, one exception to the norm was in tackling the decorative panels of pinkish-grey headers in the front wall of the Leather Bottle Inn. See *Plate 17*. These were completed ahead of the rest of the wall, the areas concerned being drawn on the card with faint pencil outlines with reference to the row of dots beneath. The pattern and its positon were determined by counting bricks on the photographs and, of course, reference to the field notes. Each pattern was then embossed, and painted to a near finished condition, before starting any of the vertical mortar lines on the rest of the wall. The reason for treating this separately was that whilst the patterns were of a different bond to the main wall, I felt they could have been too easily lost amongst all the other embossed bricks, if not identified clearly at an early stage.

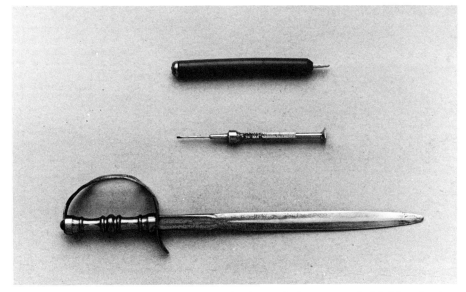

Plate 19. Embossing tools. *Top* — stone embossing tool. *Centre* — vertical brick embossing implement. *Bottom* — horizontal brick embossing implement.

STONEWORK

Fig. 27. A drawing of the card having been cut to shape, apertures removed and embossed as far as bricks and stone quoins. The subject is the shed from behind Lilac Cottage, Bishopstone, seen in Plate 20.

STONE WALLS

Stone walls can be grouped into various categories, such as, for example, *Ashlar*, smooth well-dressed stone, close fitting and often with very little mortar, commonly found in churches; *random rubble*, a pretty self explanatory name, and *rubble brought to courses*, also fairly self explanatory. Each of these types is represented in the following passages.

EMBOSSING THE CARD FOR STONEWORK

As mentioned in the field notes section, particularly recognisable stones are worth identifying and representing, but where a wall is made from reasonably consistent stones, a general impression is, I feel, satisfactory. The particularly recognisable stones may simply be quoins (corner stones) as in *Plate 20*, but it all depends on the prototype. However, sometimes all the stones in a wall are easily defined and capable of faithful reproduction on the model. The back wall of Mill Cottage, Woolstone, was just such a case and, with the information recorded on the field notes and photographs, I was able to work the chalkstone blocks around the bricked-up windows and other brick areas satisfactorily (see *Plate 21*).

With walls such as those shown in *Plates 20 & 21*, I first emboss the brickwork and then the stone quoins; for the latter I use the horizontal brick embossing tool, but this time for the verticals as well. This practice also applies to the chalkstone blocks as seen in *Plate 21*.

Once the quoins and other particularly recognizable stones have been established, the body of the wall is tackled. I use a short

Plate 20. Quoins of brick and reasonably well cut chalkstone blocks with rubble brought to courses in between.

Plate 21. The rear of Mill Cottage, Woolstone. The stone and brick area of the main building does in fact project from the original timber framed wall by 6 inches or so and was made up of overlays on the model.

Plate 22. Rubble brought to courses between brick quoins in the front wall of the stable in Denchworth. This was my first attempt at modelling a major building.

aluminium knitting needle fitted with a plastic tube handle (see *Plate 19*) to emboss the stonework. This tool has a rounded point and can be pushed in any direction on the card without tearing it, leaving behind it a depressed mortar line. I usually begin this operation at the top of the wall and work my way down, course by course. When not copying stone for stone from the photographs, I adjust the lengths of the stones to avoid the risk of producing a stone wall in perfect stretcher bond. While embossing one course the tool is not taken from the card but pushed and pulled along in a series of loops, leaving a continuous mortar line, as I hope is apparent in *Plate 22*.

For random rubble walls I vary not only the length but the overall size and shape as well, although I still work in courses to a large extent in the belief that the prototype walls were probably built layer upon layer so this must be the more convincing method to adopt. The continuous looping action with the embossing tool is not often appropriate with random rubble, especially when copying photographs. When the tool is lifted from the card, for any reason, I take great care, when starting again, to ensure it is replaced in an existing mortar groove, before carrying on.

With Canney Row, Chiseldon, there were quite a number of particularly large and recognizably shaped stones apparent (see *Plate 23*). These were picked out on the card with feint pencil lines, their positions being determined from photographs, relating the height and distance to the left or right of a window or door, for instance. After embossing, the rest of the wall was completed around them.

I find the embossed card technique excellent for Ashlar and reasonably smooth rubble walls, but stone walls are not always smooth. For those that have eroded badly, for instance, some greater texture is desirable and such treatment is considered on page 86.

Plate 23. Random rubble featuring some quite large stones. Small areas of brickwork (not apparent here) also feature on the front of Canney Row, Chiseldon.

PAINTING

The realistic appearance of a model building, in my opinion, not only depends on proto-typical architecture, which in Pendon's case comes about automatically with faithful reproduction of a prototype, but the colour-ing of the various materials used as well. Finest quality artists water colours are used almost exclusively on Pendon's village build-ings and for this reason, whenever practical, we all use absorbent materials such as card, paper, balsa wood, etc because they accept water colour nicely. The remarkable subtle 'living' tones that can be produced with the finest water colours, coupled with their superb controllability from brush to model, has made me content to look no further for other media. In many cases the pigments for artists' water colours are from suitable natural materials. For instance, the base colour for painting slates (Davy's Grey) is, I believe, actually made from ground slate.

Another advantage is that unless artists' water colours are applied very thickly, the model surfaces retain their matt finish but without seeming to be 'dead looking'. How-ever, I don't know how acrylic or oil paints behave on card or paper so I cannot make any comparison. Of course there are times when non-absorbent materials are used, simulated corrugated iron, brass tube drain pipes and the like, and in these instances I usually use matt enamels, though never straight out of tin, blends and varieties again being desirable.

The water colours I use are selected list Artists Water Colours by Winsor and Newton, and they are not excessively expen-sive. If the tops of tubes are kept on tightly they shouldn't dry up, and it pays to clean the threaded neck before replacing the cap to avoid the top jamming with paint. However, tubes can dry up and on one or two occasions I have even unwittingly bought them in this condition. I have found no answer to this problem, but I don't throw them away as there is usually plenty of usable colour left inside if the tube is cut open. I have found that when dampened, little pieces of colour that have been dug out, return to a usable con-dition. Cadmium scarlet and orange are very powerful colours, and consequently not so much is needed, yet strangely the paint that collects around the caps of these colours does not seem to dry up and I expect the two tubes I have to last me all my modelling days.

The brushes I use are also made by Winsor & Newton, I particularly like the series 16 ones for their combination of paint-holding capacity and long flexible (but not floppy)

points. For painting very fine lines, bricks, stones, timbers and interior picture painting, I use a Series 16 No. 1. No. 1 brushes from other series are kept for weathering jobs. 'The Fly By Night Brush Company's' bargain No 000 brushes are not worth buying.

For carrying water from jar to palette and mixing paint I use larger brushes kept especially for such purposes. I have some 45 palettes with ready-mixed colours, sometimes up to three different tones thinly covering the bottom of any one. My palettes are simply well washed, second-hand expanded poly-styrene food trays. (5″ long, 3½″ wide and 1″ deep) — the sort of thing supermarket foods are packaged in. Of the 45 palettes 8 of them each hold two similar brick colours, such is the variety sometimes required (as described later). With a couple of brushfuls of water, and some gentle rubbing, the colours can be restored to a workable consistency, even after having been dry for a very long time. During painting a little more water may have to be added with the best brush, but very little rubbing is then necessary.

Painting lintels and other timbers

Timbers that are built into walls are usually painted first, partly to avoid painting the mortar colour over their clean surfaces, and also to prevent any accidental slip of a timber-colour loaded brush onto a previously coloured wall, darkening a delicately painted pale area irrevocably. The mix used for timbers such as door and window frames is, of course, remembered, even labelled, for the painting of the doors themselves or further window members that should be of the same

colour (these are made at a later stage and the colours used are covered on page 27). For timbers covered with tar, creosote or com-pletely untreated, I use a mix of Charcoal Grey, Burnt Umber and a touch of Chinese White. For a tar appearance the paint can be quite thick; for slightly weathered creosote a thinner, more brown colour is, of course, required. Sometimes creosoted timbers have been so neglected that there is very little trace of colour left; for this appearance either a very thin mix is painted on, or sometimes, better still, the normal mix which, when dry, is gently rubbed in the direction of the grain, with a damp clean brush to pick up some of the paint from the surface. For untreated timbers that have weathered to an almost silver grey, the above technique is used and the process is taken even further until all that is left is the paint embedded in the grain of the card.

Painting Bricks and Mortar

The first step is to cover the brick-embossed area with mortar colour. With old lime mortar, the unweathered parts of a wall can vary from a pale cream to a light sandy brown, with perhaps just a hint of grey. The base colours I use (recommended by Roye England), are Raw Sienna, Chinese White and Charcoal Grey, obviously not very much of the latter. Varying blends of these colours are painted in different areas on the wall, making sure to get the colour down in the grooves (I use No. 0 brush). I mix the paint only just wet enough to flow into the grooves, but great care is needed because a wash can cause the card to swell excessively, which may

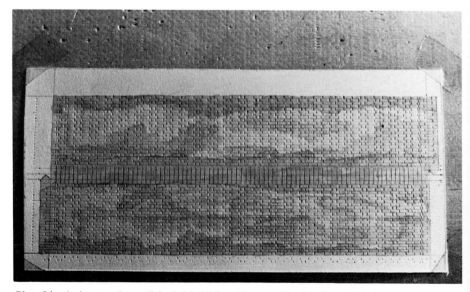

Plate 24. A short garden wall for behind Priory Cottages, Pendon Parva High Street. This picture shows blends of mortar colours in different areas.

result in a reduction of relief produced in the embossing process. Although the mortar colour I mix is not very wet, some moisture is inevitably absorbed by the card. In an area of unembossed card there is no fear that the high quality material if swelled will not return to a flat condition when dry. However, as mentioned in the embossing section, the very act of embossing creates stresses within the card, and when moistened with paint such areas often rise from the drawing board considerably. To help prevent any permanently unacceptable distortion setting in, I place a square of plate glass and a weight over the newly painted wall almost immediately. I then either find another job or go for a cup of tea until the wall is thoroughly dry.

Artists' water colours can be beautifully translucent, so that the light from the card can shine through the paint, thus giving very clear colours without necessarily being bright. If, at a later stage in painting, something appears too light, it can easily be darkened, but the opposite is nigh impossible and not recommended. The mortar colours are kept thin so that they don't affect the subsequent application of brick colour too much. The mortar colour can otherwise all too easily pick up and mix when painting each brick. Paints for bricks are selected and mixed with careful reference to the field notes and photographs for the prototype colours. The base colours I use are Light Red, Burnt Sienna, Burnt Umber, Cadmium Orange and/or Cadmium Scarlet and, on one or two occasions, Brown Madder (Alizarin).

Of course, no single colour is appropriate, and mixes of some colours with and without others are made until a satisfactory shade is produced. The shade achieved is, of course matched and assessed wet, but when the mix dries out, transformation takes place in the palette and the paint appears considerably darker. However, don't worry as in my experience this change in colour does not occur noticeably on the bricks of the model. This is probably because paint applied on the bricks is significantly thinner than the pre-mixed colour. Perhaps the light reflected from the card restores the appearance of the colour as first mixed. Incidentally, I always carry out the mixing operation, and any experimentation into the final appearance of the colours, in daylight, although I often work well into the night and actually paint bricks in a mixture of fluorescent and tungsten light.

Under artificial light the mortar colour can confuse the outline of individual bricks somewhat, and to overcome this, I arrange two, and sometimes three, bench lamps to the right of the drawing board on which the flat

beginnings of the model are still attached. These lamps shine across the surface of the card, leaving little shadows in the vertical mortar lines. This aids vision enormously.

When there are particularly dark or light bricks in the wall I always paint these first; these may be individual bricks scattered about or relatively large areas of similar colour. For a whole wall of generally similar appearance, I start painting the bricks at random from one place in a palette, changing to another but similar colour after 100 bricks or so. Although the prototype wall may appear at first glance to be made of the same colour bricks they probably vary quite subtly from one another, and the model bricks must vary in the same way.

When the brush is taken from the palette the paint on it is quite dense, so the first brick painted with it will be similarly dense. As painting progresses at random, all over the wall, the paint becomes thinner brick by brick, changing the tone slightly until no more paint will come from the brush. Then it is time to return to the palette for another brushful, and repeat the process. This subtle variation in the brick colours may seem pedantic, but I feel it is very important. It may look odd when the wall is only scattered with a few random bricks but the completed result is surprisingly effective and well worth the effort. Random colouring also overcomes the possible problem of unintended patchy areas where colour varies from the progressive depletion of the charge on the brush or unintentional variation in the mix of paint. Enough paint should be mixed initially, in the various colours required, for the painting of all the bricks on the model.

Painting individual bricks is a time-consuming business, though I find it quite a satisfying pastime. I start each one with the brush placed in the top left-hand corner and draw it to the right-hand top corner, leaving, hopefully, a straight line behind it. The brush is then drawn down a little, for the right-hand end of the brick and then to the left-hand end, lifting the brush away when I get there. The corners may require some attention if they are not already good right-angles but as the brush is supposed to have a good point, any touching up is not a problem.

The more bricks painted, the better impression of the final overall colour, and, by the time three-quarters of the wall has been completed, I may have used four different colours, each with its own range of intensity caused by the depleting charge on the brush.

At this stage I try to decide on the colours necessary to complete the wall. It may be that one of the colours already used should

predominate, or that the wall is lacking something, a browner sort of red or a more orange sort of red perhaps. It is difficult to make these decisions any earlier as too many remaining mortar coloured bricks confuse the overall impression.

For engineers blue bricks, Payne's Grey and Prussian Blue are useful base colours mixed with Charcoal Grey, Chinese White and Brown Madder (Alizarin) for darker, lighter and more mauve coloured bricks. For the decorative headers found in Vale cottages (that fall within that range) I use different mixes of the above colours. For the pinkish-

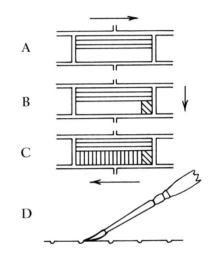

Fig. 28. Four drawings: (A) the area covered by the first brush movement, to the right; (B) the second, a downward movement; (C) the third, a movement to the left. Each brick is painted in this manner without the brush leaving the card from beginning to end. Drawing (D) gives an impression of the amount of pressure applied to the brush in order to cover at least half the brick with each longitudinal movement.

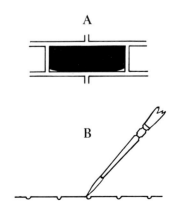

Fig. 29. (A) shows unsatisfactory (rounded) corners. (B) shows just the tip of the brush being used for touching in the corners.

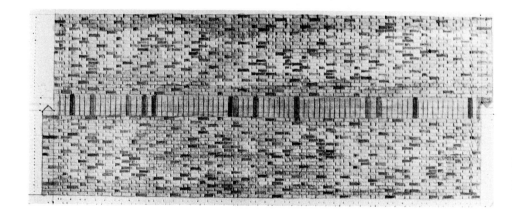

Plate 25. The Priory Cottages garden wall after 1½ hours brick painting.

Plate 26. The Priory Cottages garden wall after about four hours brick painting. It may not always take this long!

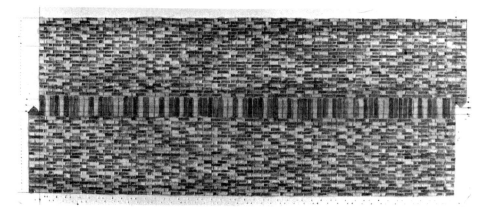

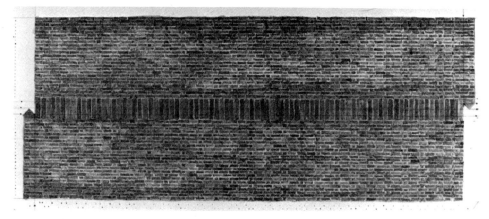

Plate 27a. The Priory Cottages garden wall again, but now with all the bricks painted. The large bricks running along the middle are capping bricks, either side of which will be a fold so the areas above and below will become opposite sides of the wall. How noticeable the mortar variations are even when largely covered with brick colours.

Plate 27b. The completed wall folded into shape.

grey ones I have used Chinese White, Davy's Grey and Cadmium Scarlet. For the dull pale yellow ones a suitable colour can be mixed from Chinese White, Raw Umber, Charcoal Grey and Aurora Yellow. Although I have never painted any common yellow bricks I have mixed what I think is a suitable colour from Chinese White, Raw Umber, Aurora Yellow and Oxide of Chromium (green). The lists of colours given in this book are useful to start a mix, but without being able to measure ingredients accurately and with infinitely variable requirements, they are of course only a guide. If only a little colour from each tube is added at one time no drastic alteration takes place, but personal experimentation and constant assessment of what you are trying to achieve (i.e. observation of the prototype) is the key to success. If you do overdo it with one colour and have to compensate with others to bring the mix back to the required shade again, all that happens is that you end up with more colour in the palette than originally intended. Not a bad thing really as it keeps well and will be used again sooner or later anyway!

Whitewashed brick walls

Whitewashed brick walls in good condition are embossed in the normal way and then, instead of being given a coat of thin mortar colour, they are given a thicker coat of whitewash colour. I usually add a touch of Raw Sienna, Charcoal Grey and Oxide of Chromium to the Chinese White to tone it down a little. For such walls in a dilapidated condition, the surfaces of some of the embossed bricks sometimes need removing carefully with the craft knife to represent eroded bricks. The wall is then given a coat of off-white whitewash colour, toned down a little more than for a wall in good condition. The eroded bricks, and others where the whitewash has merely weathered away, are treated very carefully with brick colours. Sometimes all that is needed is a feint trace of brick colour applied with a weathering brush. With very little water on the brush, if it is gently rubbed over the surface of the paint in the palette, it will of course only pick up a small amount of paint. Straight away this is gently rubbed on a piece of scrap card, until very little paint is being transferred to it, then the brush is transferred to the whitewashed wall. Keeping it fairly flat so as not to get any paint in the mortar grooves, I gently rub the brush over the desired area in a soft circular scrubbing action, which leaves the required feint trace of brick colour on the whitewash.

Having painted the brick colours over the whitewash, I have sometimes found that the

Plate 28. Brickwork was often whitewashed (and, in this view taken at East Hanney, it seems, the timbers as well!) which in my opinion is a shame, but if it has been exposed to many years of rain a very pleasing appearance is created by the brick colour showing through in varying amounts. *Pendon Museum*

edges of the bricks have appeared a little too hard or jagged. This can be remedied by very carefully floating a particularly thin greenish-grey wash all over the wall, making sure that only a very little of the existing paint is disturbed. This technique is not for those who lack confidence or experience, as the previous painting of the whole wall can just as easily be ruined as improved. I have also used this method to tone down normal brickwork that has needed softening, though again it is a very risky business.

PAINTING STONES

Painting stones is often appreciably easier than painting bricks because of their size and often irregular shape. Their colours, on the other hand, are usually considerably more difficult to reproduce. A wall consisting of stones that seem to have been quarried at the same time and place can vary even more subtly than bricks from the same brickworks.

Again for stone walls (as with brick ones) any timbers are painted first and then the mortar colour is applied to the stone-embossed card. For complete walls or just small areas of chalkstone I keep the mortar colour particularly pale as the stones themselves are often little more than off-white. If, as with many rubble chalkstone walls, the

mortar is considerably darker than the stone (see *Plate 2*. Styles Cottage Uffington), the mortar is darkened *after* the stones have been painted. If the dark mortar colour is painted quite wet, it flows into the grooves fairly easily. This may produce edges too definite for the prototype, but if this happens they can be softened by going along the edges of the mortar grooves with a damp brush of clean water, cleaning the brush on tissue and rewetting it when necessary.

For many limestones a mixture of Raw Sienna and/or Raw Umber, Chinese White and Charcoal Grey will produce a satisfactory colour. Again, as with bricks, I always mix and experiment with the colours in daylight. When painting a stone, I usually start around the perimeter and then fill in the remaining space, keeping the brush at quite a shallow angle with a little pressure applied so as to use both the body and point of the brush. This not only reduces the number of strokes needed per stone, significant when there are hundreds to paint, but a peculiar blotchy effect can otherwise result in any one stone from separate disjointed strokes. On many occasions during the painting of a stone wall, I will stop, sit back, and try to envisage the completely painted wall; a change of colour may well be thought necessary before carry-

Plate 29. The stone used for buildings in the 'Vale' varied quite considerably from area to area because of the difficulty of transport many years ago. This farm house is, I think, an example of the use of the 'Cotswold-like' stone found on the northern fringe. The moss covered stone slates on the roof would probably have come from Stonesfield. The enormous stone chimney base (almost a dormer) is interesting as are the brick chimney tops, probably a comparitively late alteration.   *Roye England*

Plate 30a. Part of the front wall of Wharf Cottage, showing quite similarly coloured stones.

ing on. When dealing with quite a pale wall remember that a considerable amount of the final tone variation and character will be created later on, at the weathering stage. It is best to resist any such temptation at this stage. A certain, and essential, amount of subtlety of stone colours will have been created by the random painting technique, as described in the brick painting section (page 21).

In the Vale, cottages often have panels of 'rag stone' built into their walls. These panels are made up of different types of stone, often with a generous amount of mortar between them. One type called Sarsenstones are usually quite rounded and a reddish brown colour; a good base colour for these is Burnt Sienna. When working on any wall, the slow build-up of colours that appear, because of the random painting technique, provides plenty of time to consider real walls, and in particular the one being copied. Again the photographs, be they colour or black and white, serve as reminders of site visits and will help bring back images that are very useful when judging colours.

Plate 30b. The Friends Meeting House, Pendon Parva, with a 'rag stone' panel with chalkstone blocks and brick reveals.

Fig. 30. A strip of card marked out, embossed and painted. The arrows point to small holes at what will be the corners. These holes serve as an accurate means of transferring the precise fold line to the reverse side of the card.

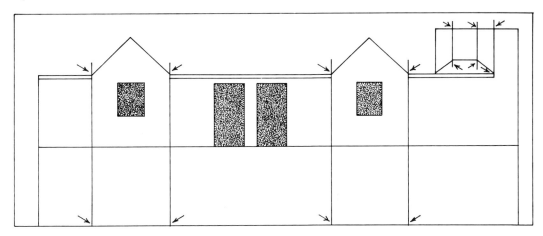

PREPARING THE CARD FOR FOLDS AND TRIMMING IT TO SHAPE

With the painting of the walls completed except for the weathering, the card can now be taken off the drawing board. The lightly pencilled corner lines (fold lines) running from the bottom of the cellar card to just above the eaves line, should now be pin pricked using a needle (mine has a wooden handle for comfort!) at the ends of the fold lines, as in *Fig. 30*.

The painted card is next placed face down on the drawing board. Although there are often many 'pin pricks' showing, the appropriate fold line holes should be quite easy to distinguish (if not, make sure you have the right ones!). The point of the craft knife should now be placed in the top one of the two holes to be joined (inside the corner) and a steel rule is then placed into position against the blade, checking that the rule is then held at the same distance from the bottom hole. The position of the rule is critical as this cut has to be accurate.

Keeping the cutting edge of the knife at quite a shallow angle to the card, I draw it along, against the rule with the blade at 90° to the card. DO NOT CUT RIGHT THROUGH, two gentle strokes are usually sufficient to make a straight line cut in the card of approximately three-quarters of its thickness only. To break through the painted surface with the knife is not catastrophic (as I have done so on a couple of occasions) but it causes enough problems to make me very careful not to! (The remedy appears later, on page 40). I usually make the vertical, three-quarter depth cuts between all the fold line 'pin pricks' before going on to the next delicate and often tricky stage. To many

Plate 31. Removing card from behind a corner to allow the card to be folded more easily.

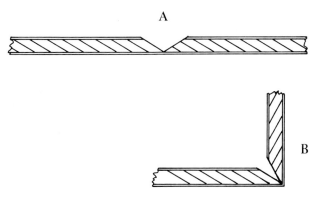

Fig. 31. A. Thickness of the card with the small vee-shaped piece of card removed. B. The card folded into a poor sort of mitre but with a continuous outer skin, the painted surface.

people this is the most difficult part of the whole process. This is to remove a thin, shallow V-shaped piece of card from between the 'pin pricks' to leave mitred edges joined only by the very thin outer surface of the card. When folded and glued this produces a strong sharpish corner. To remove the V-shaped piece, I hold the knife at between 20° and 30° to the horizontal, place the point approx 1 mm to the side of the three-quarter depth vertical cut, and draw the knife along so the very point is at the bottom of the vertical cut, as in *Plate 31*. A new blade might be wise for this operation.

These angled cuts are made all along one side of the fold lines and the whole job is then turned around to cut the other side of the V. I prefer to make both the angled cuts free-hand (as illustrated) as I concentrate on the depth of the cut rather than making a perfectly straight one, the vertical cut usually makes sure of a good straight fold. However, others may prefer to guide the knife along a steel rule. Having removed either one vee or two half-vees, the painted card is held up to a source of light, a window, or a bench lamp, to check the thickness of the layer of outer card left. If, when looking at the back, some light dimly shines through the centre of the vee cut, then sufficient card has been removed; if not, I scratch some card away with the point of the second best (rough jobs) craft knife until light does just show through. The card I use, International paste board (modern equivalent, Apsley paste board 550 microns), has two outer skins of thickish, soft white paper, between which is the paste, a grey fibrous material. To ensure a good fold, the vee cut-out has to pass through the outer paper skin and grey paste so that the pale back of the painted, front, outer skin is just visible.

Although B, in *Fig. 31*, shows the fold, I do not actually carry out the bend until much later when the model is ready to fold into a box. I prefer to make the fold only once, as even a very few repeated folding actions can open the grain of the card's vulnerable outer skin with the result that little splits become apparent.

With the confidence that the corners will fold satisfactorily, I then cut away the margin of card from around the painted area, using craft knife and steel rule; if laying the rule over painted areas is unavoidable, a sheet of clean paper is used to protect the delicately created surface. Removal of the margins is best done at this stage as the card strip is still of a single thickness; glued-on door and window components would prevent the sheet laying flat on the cutting board.

A PAUSE FOR THOUGHT

Some consideration of the rooms to be furnished and illuminated (if this is to be undertaken) is necessary before going further, as they have a bearing on the doors, windows and floors. Standard procedure at Pendon is that at least one room should be illuminated. In my case, the things that have actually been illuminated range from the back of a drawn curtain to a fully furnished room consisting of 40 or more hours work. In every case some ventilation is required as our usual source of light, a 3 volt torch bulb, also produces heat which must be allowed an escape route. In the past I have expected this heat to find its way out through purposely built-in gaps around the glazing material. This may or may not work as, I am afraid only time will tell. Some of the earlier cottage models, built in the 1950s (not by me) now show signs of condensation stains on the insides of the glazing material, presumably because of inadequate ventilation. To be on the safe side, I now model an open window in or above the rooms that are illuminated. So the decisions as to which window frames should be modelled to accept an open window (one of the very last jobs) goes hand in hand with the choice of which rooms are to be furnished and/or just illuminated. The same applies to doors — it may be desirable to model a particular door open, to give a better view of a fully furnished room.

As mentioned earlier, the conventional method of illumination has been by means of a torch bulb and for the light to reach the desired places there must be a ducting of some sort, which usually means incorporating a card box tube in the internal structure, i.e. through the floors. This tube is best placed toward the centre of the model, as light from the bulb has a nasty habit of showing through the rather thin card walls, if placed at all close.

More about the floors, internal structure, furnishings and room illumination can be found in the section on page 35, but with these considerations borne in mind I carry on with the next stage — doors and windows.

Roye England

DOORS *and* WINDOWS

Good clean cuts in the card are always desirable but it is with doors and windows that cut edges are most often seen; raised edges with a torn appearance look exactly what they are. As the door and window frames I represent are usually made from nicely sawn timber, neatly cut card is a must. Although I have not always succeeded (as some of the photographs show), I find the following procedure helps me attain a reasonable standard. The knife I use (with Swan Morton No 1 blades) seems to produce less raised edges if held at a shallow angle to the card.

The condition of the blade also makes a contribution, and again a new blade is essential and may only last for the cutting of one or two windows, before being either discarded or relegated to the 'rough jobs knife handle'. If a little raised edge does appear I restore it by rubbing the back of a finger-nail along the edge. If you are using a nicely rounded metal scalpel handle with no sharp edges etc, this can also be laid on its side and rubbed along the offending edge to flatten any burr.

Most doors have a frame of some sort; if flush with the wall, I include it in the wall card, if not, I make a separate frame to be glued behind the wall. A rectangle of suitable thickness card is cut to be some 5 mm larger all round than the aperture in the wall. It is then held behind the wall card and a very sharp pencil is run along the aperture edges to provide an accurate outline on the door frame card (see *Fig. 33*). From this outline I mark the inside edge of the frame, usually about 1 mm from the sides and top, the bottom line of the aperture outline completing the rectangle to be cut away (see *Fig. 33*). The frame, its edges and a little of the margin are then painted and left to dry.

A little white PVA glue is then brushed on to the unpainted area of the margin, (too much and it will squeeze out onto the painted and visible part of the frame) and the frame is then positioned behind the wall card, placed on a small piece of plate glass and compressed by a flat steel weight I have for just this purpose. Ten minutes or so should be sufficient for the job to set.

I make plain planked doors using a piece of 0.75 mm card, cut with at least a 5 mm margin outside the frame aperture size for securing it. Again this is held in position behind the frame aperture and the outline on the door marked on the card with a sharp

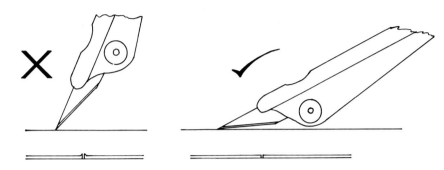

Fig. 32. *Holding the knife at a shallow angle to the card seems to produce a clean cut.*

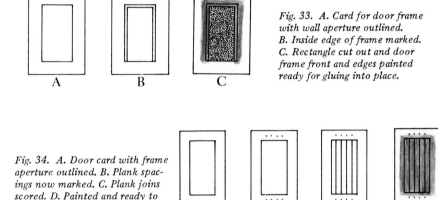

Fig. 33. *A. Card for door frame with wall aperture outlined. B. Inside edge of frame marked. C. Rectangle cut out and door frame front and edges painted ready for gluing into place.*

Fig. 34. *A. Door card with frame aperture outlined. B. Plank spacings now marked. C. Plank joins scored. D. Painted and ready to be glued into place.*

pencil. The plank spacings (often 2 mm) are then marked in the top and bottom margins and the plank joins are then scored using the horizontal brick embossing tool against a steel rule adjusted to the spacing marks. The scored door is then painted, including some of the margin to ensure that none of the white card will show.

The rural 1930s doors that I am usually concerned with were painted in dull colours, often greens or browns. On only one occasion have I had to represent a door with a two tone colour scheme, Mill Cottage Woolstone, where period photographs showed quite pale panels.

Two coats of paint are usually necessary for good coverage plus some weathering variation which greatly improves an otherwise all over single colour appearance. Contrary to normal practice, the weathering is done before the door is glued into place, otherwise it is difficult to get into the corners and edges against the frame. When all the painting is done, the card is glued into place,

taking care that the scored area is central in the aperture and that the planks are upright, unless, of course, the door has settled, in which case the frame may not have right-angled corners and other such adjustments will have to be incorporated. When satisfied with the alignment, I sandwich the job between glass and a steel weight.

The inside of a door does not usually concern me at this stage, for, although the prototypical bracing may need to be represented in an illuminated room, this detailing work is most often done as a dummy door on the wall of the interior, which is for quite a time removable from the main model.

I make framed and panelled doors by holding a piece of good quality cartridge paper behind the frame aperture and marking its outline on the paper. Measuring from the aperture outline, I pencil in the outlines of the panels, and then cut them out. This fret is then carefully glued to a piece of 0.75 mm card of the same overall size. If the panels are to be a different colour to the framing fret, the

Fig. 35. A. Paper with aperture outline. B. Paper with panel edges marked. C. Panel spaces cut out. D. Framing fret painted. E. Backing (panel) card. F. Panels painted on backing card. G. Paper fret and card backing glued together ready to be fixed behind wall card.

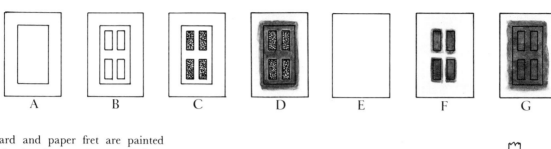

A   B   C   D   E   F   G

backing card and paper fret are painted separately in the chosen colours and then, when dry, glued together and later fixed behind the wall card.

Doors modelled ajar or wide open are quite simple to make. A piece of card is cut to door size plus 5 mm extra on the hinge side. Planks or panels are represented as usual and then a knife cut is made (on the outside for doors that open inwards and vice versa) along the hinge line, cutting into the card for approximately two-thirds of its thickness. The card is then folded along the hinge line. The open vee along the hinge line, of course, needs some paint before the 5 mm extra tab of card is glued behind the wall.

DOOR FITTINGS

Shed-like doors often have large strap hinges visible and these can be made from thin paper using a small rectangular piece (to be glued on the door frame) and a longer tapering piece for the door itself. Alternatively a one-piece hinge can be useful to actually 'hang' a gate for instance. These bits of paper have their edges and outer sides painted before being fixed in place. The minute amounts of white PVA used do not adhere to the paint-work very well unless the places where they are to be affixed are dampened with a little water from a brush. The glue is also more controllable in these minute quantities if it is diluted a little with water before being applied to the paper components. Holding the pieces of paper in tweezers, I touch them on to an area of diluted glue on an old tin lid. If some glue oozes out from under the paper when it has been gently pressed into place on the model, I let it get tacky, then scrape it off the door with the craft knife, any damage to the door paint can be touched up with door colour, or a bit of rust colour, often seen below exposed hinges, bolts and the like. However, it is obviously best to be very careful not to damage the paintwork.

Door latches, as in *Plate 32*, are made from copper wire and steel wire, bent and fitted into two holes made in the door. The latch

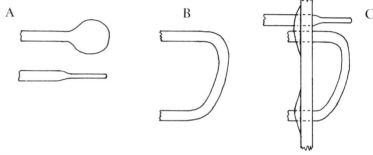

Fig. 36. A. Copper wire squashed and filed (if needed) to shape for latch thumb piece. B. Steel wire bent to shape of handle. C. The wire components pushed through the door and secured with Evo-Stik.

release is made from copper wire that has been squashed flat at one end. The handle is made from steel wire. Why steel? It stays put when bent, and I happen to have a stock of it!

The steel wire is bent to shape in a pair of tweezers and then pushed gently against the door, leaving two marks to indicate the positions of the holes. The two holes are either made with a needle in a wooden handle or a small drill in a pin chuck, it really depends on which is to hand. The top hole is made large enough to accommodate the top end of the steel loop as well as the copper thumb piece. After being pushed into the holes, the metal parts are secured on the inside with a dab of Impact Evo-Stick (not used as an impact

Plate 32. Copper and steel wire door latch.

adhesive though, but just as a glue that sticks metal fairly well). The handle and thumb piece are then painted with matt Humbrol, along with a rectangular area around them which is to represent the plate that is commonly a part of such latches. The common or front door knob is represented by a shortened brass pin with a much filed down head, painted, pushed into a suitable hole and secured behind. Keyholes are no more than a pin prick and a dab of paint.

I am afraid I have next to no experience of plain or ornamental door knockers and letter boxes so I cannot describe how to make them. Plain ones by implication should not be very difficult to suggest at least, but fancy ones I think I would be inclined to leave alone, after all their omission will probably not greatly alter the character of the building.

Weather boards at the bottoms of doors usually consist of a piece of thick card cut to a wedge shape, the cut surface being glued to the door before painting. On a few occasions I have had to build doors incorporating windows, although I can't recall the detail. I seem to remember two methods being employed on such jobs. On one I had cut the window aperture in the door and then realised that, if I had glued a piece of clear acetate sheet behind the door, the glazing would appear set back too far, because of the thickness of the card. To remedy this I removed some card from around the aperture on the back of the door, and let a small square of glazing material into the rebate. However, now I would cut the glazing to size and fit the acetate a little way into the aperture, securing it with only a spot of glue. Beading to secure the glazing (whether it should be there or not) would probably look a bit on the heavy side and is better left off. Another alternative that might suit some modellers is to make the door out of the glazing material and use a paper overlay attached with Spray Mount to represent planking, etc. It is all a matter of choice.

WINDOWS

Modern etched brass window frames on the whole look very good, but, in the buildings with which I am concerned, each window is probably unique, so 'off the shelf' standard sized repetitive styles are not appropriate and hand-made windows are unavoidable. Unfortunately, my construction methods are sometimes a bit too obvious, especially when the overlap of the paper glazing bars are viewed obliquely. However, I can live with these imperfections for, although I strive for accuracy in details, they are not in my mind, there to be singled out. They simply enhance

Roye England

a building when viewed as a whole and, when seen in their settings, the windows should not be any more striking than other parts of the building.

For closed casement window frames (if not already included in the wall card), I cut a piece of 0.2 mm card large enough to include a margin of approx 5 mm all round the aperture. As with doorframes, this card is then held behind the wall card and on it is pencilled the aperture outline. Measuring from the outline I then pencil lines to indicate the inside edges of the window frame. These lines may be no more than ⅔ mm from the wall outline and if a double window is required then a central upright is included.

Having cut away the unwanted card, (see page 12) the frame is painted. The 5 mm margin then receives a thin coating of white PVA before being positioned accurately behind the main wall card. The job is then sandwiched between glass plates and weighted to assure a good bond. After five minutes or so I lift the weight and glass off to see if I had applied too much glue which may have been squeezed out onto the visible part of the frame. This does not often happen as I am well practised at judging the amount of glue required! However, mistakes sometimes happen and with an interval of no more than five minutes, the glue will still be soft enough to be gently scraped away with the craft knife (or scrap card) without doing any damage. Afterwards the job is returned to the glass

sandwich and weighted for perhaps another ten minutes. When set, I next apply the glazing bars. These are made from good quality cartridge paper cut on plate glass with a steel rule held parallel with the sheet's edge approximately ½ mm in. The thickness of the knife blade takes up part of the ½ mm and, when the knife is gently drawn along against the straight edge, at a shallow angle, a strip of paper less than ½ mm wide will be produced. If the knife blade is not held at a shallow angle, a thin crumpled paper spiral will probably be produced. I mark where the glazing bars are to be glued on the back of the card, but I do not take all that much care over the accuracy of these marks as the final alignment is carried out when the bars are attached to the frame card.

I cannot think of the reason why (I feel there must be one), but I usually fix the vertical bars first. A small blob of PVA is positioned, with an old paint brush, on the pencil marks, then, with a glazing bar in tweezers, one end of the paper is gently pushed into its blob of glue — and then the other. To make sure that the glazing bar is vertical, I turn the job over to view the painted side and then hold it in front of a dark background so that when I am judging the window spacings the glazing bars show up very clearly. I can then say to myself, 'top, left a bit', or 'bottom, right a bit', remembering that when I turn the job over, the actual prodding of the glued end will have to be in the opposite direction. This task has to be carried out fairly swiftly as the tiny quantity of glue 'goes off' very quickly. As the tweezers are usually still quite handy, I use them to do the prodding and any glue that might stick to them is easily removed. After I am satisfied with the alignment, I press the glued end firmly down onto the frame card with what one could call the butt end of the tweezers.

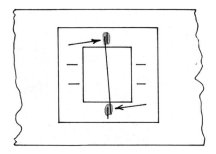

Fig. 38. The inside surface of the main wall card with the window frame attached and glazing bar needing to be prodded into an acceptable alignment.

The horizontal bars are fixed in much the same way but, in the case of a double window, a small blob of glue is included on the middle upright. The fixing of the bars where they cross is done after alignment and when the glue at the bar ends has set. I then apply a small quantity of very slightly dilute PVA to the rear of the cross. (I keep my glue brush suspended in a jam jar of water to stop it getting clogged up. When I take the brush from the pot to the patch of glue that I have squeezed onto an old tin lid, I can brush off as much of the water on the edge of the jar and carry as little as I choose to the glue, to dilute it.) Being applied to the rear, the glue does not create any painting problems, although it is left to well and truly set before the glazing bars are painted.

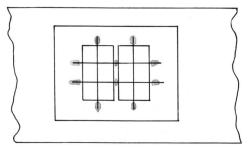

Fig. 39. Window frame card with glazing bars attached.

Plate 33. Casement window in the left-hand end of The Leather Bottle Inn. The painted line down the middle upright does not look quite as bad from a more normal viewing distance.

I paint the bars at this stage to avoid the possibility of getting any paint on the glazing. I do not have the water colour very runny for this job, as on one occasion the bars expanded quite alarmingly and did not dry out to the original and desired position.

Glazing comes next and I normally use approximately 15 thou acetate sheet. I don't know that acetate is any better than any other materials but it does not seem to get scratched too badly in handling and appears sufficiently stable not to warp later. As the glazing bars and the glue that attaches them project a little from the frame card, the acetate cannot be fixed easily to the frame card. To overcome this problem I cut little rectangles of cartridge paper as packing pieces and glue them between the glazing bar ends, as in *Fig. 40.*

I then cut a piece of acetate sheet to size, so that its edges, when put in place, run along the centres of the packing pieces. To hold the acetate in place, I use PVA, although this glue probably does not adhere very well to the shiny, non-porous surface. However, I use the glue to create a socket around and over the sheet's edges. The advantage of using PVA is that it doesn't string and there is no risk of plastic type glue or thin solvent spoiling the window's appearance.

Of course, sash windows, for instance, are more difficult. The first ones I had to represent were for the model of Wharf Cottage, Uffington, the seventh model I built for Pendon (in June 1982). These were made up

from several layers of 0.2 mm card, using the same paper glazing bar and glazing attachment techniques as before.

The window shown in *Plate 33* needed to have its frame flush with the planking. This

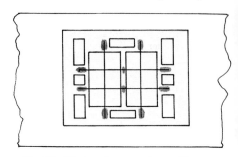

Fig. 40. Window frame card, cartridge paper glazing bars and paper packing pieces glued in place.

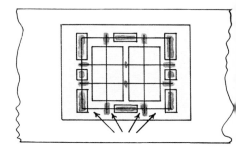

Fig. 41. Acetate sheet held in place with PVA. Gaps left for ventilation (to allow heat from any interior illumination to escape).

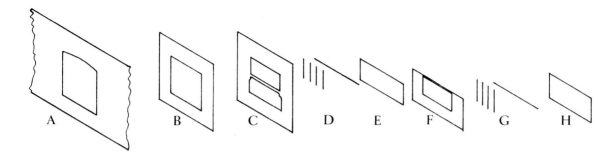

Fig. 42. A. Main wall card with arch-topped aperture. B. 0.2mm card for frame, sash track and arch cut off. C. Top sash and sash track sides. D. Glazing bars for top sash. E. Acetate for top sash. F. Three-sided frame for bottom sash. G. Glazing bars for bottom sash. H. Acetate for bottom sash. A, B, C, D, etc. was also the order of assembly.

was arranged by making a card box (which incorporates the brickwork seen below the planks) approximately 2 mm smaller than the overall dimensions across the planking and onto which a fully glazed window frame was glued over a pre-cut aperture. The planks were then glued up to the frame's edges. The thickness of the frame card, glazing bar and glazing materials, when fixed together, had to match the amount that the overlapping weather boards would project.

I produce leaded-light windows by scratching the pattern of lead in the outward facing surface of the acetate glazing material. This is done before cutting the required size from the sheet stock. If a small, window-sized piece is cut out first, it is almost impossible to stop it moving about under the steel rule while using the scratching tool. I normally use the needle in wooden handle 'pin pricking' tool (seen in *Plate 31*) to scratch grooves which are later filled with paint to represent the lead. After the window has been cut from the stock sheet, I paint it with matt Humbrol (GWR wagon grey), and before it has completely dried, I pick off the paint from between the lead lines with paper tissue wrapped over the end of an old paint brush handle. The stubborn little patches that sometimes remain (I don't rub too hard with the tissue as I want to leave the paint down in the grooves) are encouraged to disappear by gently stroking them with a small paint brush, just damp with thinners; some mopping with tissue may be necessary afterwards for a good clean job.

I used to make a paper frame, glazing bar and acetate sandwich for open casement windows but they would often be viewed in such a way that the somewhat overscale thickness of the frame would be seen. Now I

paint the frame on the glazing. I begin by marking out a rectangle on approximately 25 thou acetate including the area of the window frame and on this scratch grooves to represent the glazing bars and slightly roughen the surrounding frame areas with the needle. When cut from the stock sheet the rectangle is painted (usually white) in the way leaded lights are painted, but this time including the framework. I do not fit the open windows until the whole model is virtually complete, as they can easily be damaged or may even inhibit the construction of other features, thatching, for instance; the trimming of thatch can be difficult enough, without working around an out-swung window. When I do

Plate 34. Sash window in central section of Wharf Cottage. At a viewing distance of, say, 3 ft, the glazing bar alignment and the holes in the curtains are far less apparent.

Plate 35. Leaded-light windows in the front of Stephen Williams' model of Hinton Parva School, which is now in Pendon Parva High Street. Unfortunately, all the leaded-light windows I have made are in models now fixed in position in Pendon's Vale scene and no longer accessible for photography.

fix them in place I use Impact Evo-Stik (a bit messy in my opinion) for a trustworthy bond.

Although I have not yet needed to model any stained glass, I have experimented with (I think) very promising results, on the back of a piece of leaded light (scratched and painted acetate) painting the areas between the lead lines with different Humbrol colours well thinned down. This technique could come in very handy for church and Victorian front door windows alike.

Interior window sills and reveals sometimes need to be modelled in brick-walled buildings, but more commonly (or more unavoidably!) it is stone-walled buildings that need them. With brick and timber-walled buildings I feel the layers of window card, paper and acetate make up a sufficient thickness, but for thick walls I glue three pieces of card on edge around the window, as in *Fig. 43*, pre-painted with the room colour.

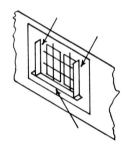

Fig. 43. Three pieces of card glued around the window as sill and reveals. The sill of course is very convenient for ornaments or flowers.

In the old days Roye used to make curtains from ribbon, but over the years (30 or more) they have in some cases, rotted badly, leaving a very poor apology. He has since used toffee papers (a bit shiny sometimes) but now favours painted Kleenex tissue — Kleenex rather than Fly By Night Hankies Inc. tissue because it is reputed to be acid free, and so presumably will not eat itself away. So I use Kleenex too, unpainted or just slightly tinted a creamy colour, for thick old net curtains or grey for dirty ones. These are glued on the acetate locating/packing pieces. I sometimes cover the whole window with net but I also have occasion to cover only the bottom half, as you may have noticed in some of the photographs. I have even painted little white dots in a pattern on the tissue to represent a woven design in the net but without much success, they should, after all, only be notice-able at very close range.

For ordinary curtains, I glue a strip of painted tissue down each side of the window, either straight over the acetate or onto the reveal card. I paint the tissue on both sides,

Plate 36a. It seems to have been common practice in the 'Vale' to have only the upstairs windows open, as all of them are here.   *Roye England*

for good coverage, with fairly nondescript dull colours, appropriate to Pendon's period and because, although the curtains should be visible, I don't think they should be at all striking. I sometimes paint coloured patterns over an undercoat for variety, dots, stripes or a flowery sort of pattern — very satisfying when they come out well.

I have on occasion felt that some window fittings were needed, for example I have painted casement latch handles on the inside of the acetate, and even glued a thin strip of paper from window to ledge to represent the stay of an open casement.

Cobwebs are often quite prominent in outhouse and shed windows, and these can be painted on the inside of the acetate with a dryish whitish water colour mix, gently stip-pled into place for the general covering type of web, or a little triangular shape for the separate corner bracket type web. Sometimes I have also suggested the shape of the cart-wheel type.

The types of window I have covered here do not of course include all variations but the principles can be applied to many types. For very intricate ones perhaps some of the proprietary etchings might coincide with your needs. Of course if you happen to be a photo-etcher yourself, or know someone who could do the job for you, etched frames are much easier!

Plate 36b. An open window in the Old Vicarage.

ASSEMBLY

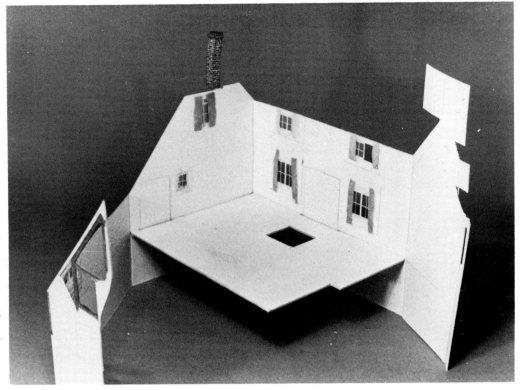

Plate 37a. Willis' Cottage with two walls glued to the ground line floor, which has a light shaft hole cut in it. The extra door and window frame cards can be seen inside the walls, as can the painted tissue curtains.

FOLDING INTO A BOX

While the model is still a long strip of card, I mark a floor line all along the card (inside) and then fold. The corners should hinge easily if enough card has been removed from behind the fold line. With two folds made, I measure the distance between two opposite surfaces and so on around the inside of the card, as in *Fig. 44.*

The dimensions are transferred to a sheet of 0.75 mm card which will form a floor at approximately ground level. When cut out, the floor is tried in position with the model walls wrapped around it (internal structures *don't have* to be made from pasteboard but in my case they are). If it is a good fit you can think yourself very lucky — more often than not a little trimming is required, but be careful for it is easier to trim the existing one than make another if it is too small. When an accurate fit has been achieved, I make an exact copy that will later be glued approximately 2 mm from the bottom of the cellar.

Before fitting I now think back to the light shaft planning stage (page 26) and cut a hole in each floor card approximately 18 mm square at the pre-planned position.

When fitting I brush a bead of PVA along the ground floor line on two adjacent walls, place the floor card in position and sit there —

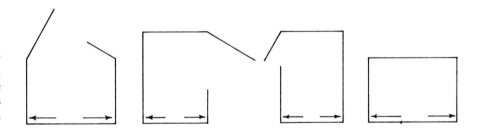

Fig. 44. These four dimensions are sufficient to construct a floor plan, as long as there are a couple of right angles involved.

patiently holding and inspecting it for a correct setting, This can take between five and ten minutes. I have tried other ways, all four sides at once, with corner protectors and side spacers held by an elastic band around the whole building. However, holding power required meant the use of an elastic band which was not much bigger than the model, and was very difficult to position correctly. Because the glue was setting all the time and the band was gripping so tightly, I did not get much chance to make the slight adjustments that were necessary — all in all not a very satisfactory state of affairs and not attempted again.

I prefer to hold the walls to the floor by hand. One wall is horizontal on a glass plate,

the other vertical; one hand gently pushes the floor against each wall while the other hand is held against the outside of the vertical wall, protected against finger prints with a piece of tissue. Maybe it goes without saying, but anyway, during this procedure I am careful not to let my fingers stray from ground level, as a finger pushing in a window space could have very regrettable consequences. From time to time I check that the job is setting squarely by placing the model upright on a plate of glass. If it has a tendency to twist, another slight twist in the opposite direction will usually correct it. The structure is then held firmly on the glass for a little while, as the glue continues to set, still keeping the walls in good contact with the floor card.

Plate 37b.

I carry on with this procedure all round the model and then fit internal strengtheners at the corners and across the underside of the floor. The cross members are all of the same depth (25 mm or so), their bottom edges providing a level base to which the copy of the floor card is glued. The completed cellar base is subsequently strong enough to withstand the considerable handling it will receive during further construction.

Plate 37c.

Plate 38. Willis' Cottage, lying on its back with the cellar base floor in front. Corner braces and cross members are visible within the cellar walls. The cellar base floor will be glued to the cross members and the cellar walls.

INTERIORS

The majority of Pendon buildings have furnished interiors, especially those arranged nearest to the visitors. The furnished rooms can only be seen by specially arranged parties these days as plunging the Museum corridors into sudden darkness is not acceptable during normal opening hours.

The furnishings in some of the models have been based upon period pieces found in the prototypes. Sometimes these are taken from period photographs in books, but mostly from my own home! The telephone I made for my latest room was based on photographs of GWR offices in J. K. L. Russell's book *GWR Company Servants* which showed just the sort of prototype I was looking for.

I normally start by cutting four pieces of 0.75 mm card, three walls and a floor. These, when finally fixed together, will make a room (detachable for the time being) to be placed inside the model behind the chosen window

Plate 39. Part of an interior I made for The Leather Bottle Inn. During the construction of the building its planned eventual location in the museum was changed to a more distant position some six to eight feet from the visitors. Because of this decision I made a quick copy for the inside of the model and kept the more time-consuming original (illustrated) for separate display.

Plate 40. How valuable photographs such as this one are these days, not just for modelling purposes.
Roye England

as can be seen in *Plate 41a*. The card floors have been painted to represent such things as quarry tiles, stone flags and congoleum squares (a lino sort of product of the period) and carpets of painted filter paper and rag rugs of roughed up and painted filter paper have been glued on top. The walls are often painted single plain colours — some surprisingly gaudy to my modern eyes but I'm told that's how they often were. Wallpapers of various designs are another challenge and sometimes wooden panelling is represented by scoring and painting around the bottom halves of the walls. Interior doors are produced in the same way as exterior ones.

I have modelled sideboards, Welsh dressers, tables, chairs, etc using veneers, card and paper — often a mixture. The artefacts that appear standing on such items of furniture include brass tube and glass bead table lamps, dished paper disc bowls with paper flowers, a card and plasticine horned record player, many paper disc plates (cut by leather punch), card tin boxes, card books and of course paper newspapers. On the Welsh dresser, shown in *Plate 39*, there are cups made from the ends of cocktail sticks and jars of jam from fibre optic. A wheel-back dining chair I made for my latest interior has a card seat, wooden legs, a copper wire back arch and steel wire stays. Easy chairs (quite difficult I think) have been carved from solid balsa followed by a coat of fairly runny interior grade Polyfilla, which when dry is painted with water colour. Cast iron ranges and

Plate 41a. Looking down into the partly built Old Vicarage, showing two furnished rooms next to their respective light shafts. I had quite a lot of trouble with both shafts as they are made far too close to the outside walls. During an early check with battery and bulb, I found that an unacceptable amount of light was escaping from the continuation of the box tube shaft (not shown) only to shine through the outside walls. To resolve the problem I sheathed the shaft with baking foil, a great deal of additional effort that could easily have been avoided by incorporating the light shafts nearer the centre of the building.

grates have been made from folded card well rubbed with a very soft black pencil. The old fashioned telephone I mentioned earlier was made from three pieces of nickel silver turned in a lathe — stem-cum-base, mouthpiece and earpiece. These, along with a very thin piece of copper wire, were soldered together and then painted. Some of the later vases were also made from turned nickel silver, quite an improvement on my earlier technique of making them from old paint brush handles.

The various types of clock I have made have all been based on real ones, American hanging wall clocks, Edwardian mantelpiece clocks and of course the old favourite, the grandfather clock. A card body was made in each case painted with the appropriate colour. The clock faces are glazed with discs of acetate, the edges of which are painted with Humbrol gold to represent the brass bezel. The late evening time at Pendon Parva is very nearly pub chucking out time i.e. 10.05 p.m. Having mentioned the grandfather clock as being an old favourite, I must stress how easy it is to make the interiors of all sitting rooms too similar. The same can happen with kitchens and dining rooms (I have yet to make a bedroom or loo interior) and in my case I am a little guilty of making them too 'Middly Classy'. I remember one of Pendon's cottage modellers, Penny Thompson, over-coming this problem in a most commendable fashion. If you ever get the chance, take a close look at the interior of Keepers Cottage at the beginning of the village green in Pendon Parva. I stole a look inside before the model had been set in the scenery. The plain work-a-day atmosphere she has captured is

just what my work-a-day interiors lack. Only one of mine has come anywhere near it, that is the kitchen/dining/living room in my recon-struction of the ex Friends Meeting House. This has old coats hanging from hooks on the wall. These are made from carved balsa covered with paper tissue and painted. Also hanging on the wall is a game bag, and on the table some cloth, paper, a can of oil and a double barrelled (12 bore, hammer action)

shot gun. These items did a lot towards creating the atmosphere of an estate worker's, sometimes poacher's, most used room. Strange he should leave the curtains open for all-and-sundry to look at the evidence of his intent, if not the actual plunder of his activities.

Some of the details I have just been describing can only be for the modeller's personal satisfaction — after all we do like to

Plate 41b. This 'middle class' drawing room-cum-study is another interior that was replaced in the model building by a short-cut version. After sixty hours of work I could not bring myself to lose many of the details by having the room only viewable through two comparatively small windows. So this one is also on show separately. The aspidistra has folded and painted paper leaves glued to a paint brush handle bowl. Some of the paintings are original water colour pictures while others are copied from record sleeves and the like. Three are copies from L. T. C. Rolt's biography of Brunel: The SS *Great Britain* on its maiden voyage, Clifton suspension bridge, and Mrs. I. K. Brunel. Just visible in the fireplace is a shim brass fire screen with a sailing ship design embossed upon it.

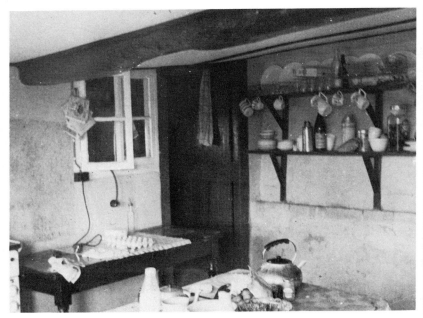

Plate 42a. Although not taken in the '30s, there is much of the period in evidence. *Roye England*

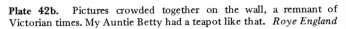

Plate 42b. Pictures crowded together on the wall, a remnant of Victorian times. My Auntie Betty had a teapot like that. *Roye England*

Plate 42c. What a floor — definitely not 'middly classy'.
Roye England

Plate 42d. How things have changed. The tea service would be hidden away in a cupboard nowadays, but these people were obviously very proud of theirs. I wonder what the umbrella/walking stick holder is made of? *Roye England*

show off our work, so, for the rooms to be appreciated by the visitors they need some internal illumination. This is achieved by means of a torch bulb and card tube ducting (Roye's method), much to the disgust of Stewart Hine, whose piped light system illuminates Pendon's lighted train. Stewart's piped light system is based on the total internal reflection properties of sheet perspex and I admit that it is probably easily adaptable to cottage lighting. However, I have not, so far, tried it. Fibre optics are yet another possibility I may get round to trying in the future.

I let the light into the rooms via holes in the ceiling, which are fed with light from a nearby shaft accommodating a torch bulb. When satisfied with the appearance of the furnished room (viewed through the window) I glue it in place to the sub-floor. Next comes the ceiling with a hole in it, the size of the hole depending on how far away the bulb will be. I am only concerned with simulating oil lamp light so I do not usually need a very large aperture, approx 6 mm square seems to be quite adequate. The positioning of the aperture needs consideration as the viewer should not be able to see exactly where the light is coming from. I temporarily glue the ceiling to the top edges of the room walls with just one or two spots of glue, then, if I have not already done so, I complete the lined tube between the ground line and cellar base floors. Three sides of this tube are continued to approximately 10 mm above the ceiling height, whilst the fourth stops flush with the ceiling. Horizontal light tube (as opposed to what I should perhaps have been calling the bulb tube) sides are then glued across the top of the ceiling card, ending either side of the aperture, with a stop-end, if needed.

Lids to the bulb tube and the horizontal light tube are then made and temporarily glued in place so that a test can be carried out with a lighted bulb positioned in the shaft. Leaking light from the temporary joints has to be ignored at this stage as we are really only concerned with confirming that the hole in the ceiling has been satisfactorily placed. If a little too much light streams into the room, the bulb can be lowered in the shaft to weaken its effect. If all is well, carefully dismantle the temporary joints and reassemble the structure permanently. As all the card assemblies made inside the model only have butt joints the corners of the lighting shafts and illuminated rooms can leak quite a lot of light. This problem can be overcome by gluing opaque black paper over the joints.

After more internal strengtheners have been glued in place, I also paint the rooms

Plate 43. Looking down at the upstairs floor/downstairs ceiling of Willis' Cottage. In the centre of the white area is the bulb shaft, to the right is the horizontal light tube leading to the ceiling aperture and to the left the beginnings of a short-cut type of bedroom. The two upright pieces of card seen in the room are light baffles to prevent the viewer directly seeing the source of light. The roundabout way in which the light reaches the viewer's eye makes for better light diffusion. Note the solid balsa infill of the left-hand chimney.

Plate 44. Two bulb shafts and horizontal light tubes in the Old Vicarage model (painted with stripes for easy identification in this photograph. I usually paint them all over black.

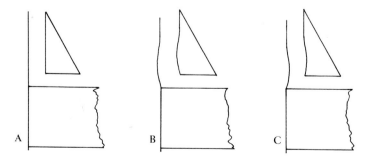

Fig. 45. Card buttresses glued inside the model to both the floor and wall. A. for an upright wall, B. for a bulging one, and C. for one that curves inwards.

that are not furnished, all over black, as rooms in prototype houses often appear very dark, even in broad daylight. Quite often the walls of old buildings bulge fairly noticeably and on rare occasions even curve inwards. To represent any such features I glue internal buttresses cut to the correct profile, as in *Fig. 45*.

At this stage I also glue in card partitions between the walls. They not only help to keep the walls in place but also provide a convenient means of fixing the ceilings. If the upper ceilings are nice and level they greatly assist in the manufacture and fitting of roof profiles.

For wavy or flat roofs, I begin the support structure with a central spine of card running from upper ceiling to ridge. The line of the ridge should include any undulations (or sagging) of the prototype as well as any angled hip or half-hip ends. Triangular buttress type profiles are then glued to the spine and ceiling. For an old wavy roof that sags between the rafters, varying profiles will be necessary, glued in sequence along the roof space, as in *Plate 46*. Roye England has achieved the same effect by gluing chamfered

Plate 45. The rear of the Old Vicarage with upper ceilings glued in place and the beginnings of the roof structure, two ridge spines, one with chimney, and the odd roof profile.

overlays of card on to the main roof card for the tiles to rise and fall over.

I find a thin card/thick paper skin blended with and glued over varying profiles is the most satisfactory method to achieve the uneven effect of an ageing roof, although some local bumps could best be modelled using a small chamfered overlay as well.

Plate 46. The Old Vicarage with varying roof profiles placed to make a series of waves in one place and more subtle undulations in others.

ROOFS

CHIMNEYS

Chimneys which sprout from the ridge have to be catered for in the main ridge spine. For chimney stacks in fairly good condition I lay out the dimensions of the prototype on a sheet of 0.6 mm pasteboard, bearing in mind, on which side of the model the corner joint will come (preferably out of sight given normal viewing). The card is then marked out and the bricks or stones embossed in the normal way and the visible areas painted.

Above and below the painted area I prick through the corner/fold lines and then carry out the vee of card removing technique at the back. The chimney is then cut out from the stock sheet, leaving if possible, some 25 mm or so beneath the visible area. The outside edges that will come together as the corner joint are bevelled off to form a mitre before the card is folded into a tube. I then measure the inside dimensions of the tube and shape a piece of balsa wood to be a good fit inside. The piece of balsa is made long enough to fill the tube from the bottom to within 5 or 6 mm of the top. Glue is then brushed on three adjacent inner sides of the card which are then folded around the balsa. While the assembly is drying the card can be held to the balsa between the thick ends of two engineer's squares, with the job on a plate of glass. The final side is best glued when these three sides have set; this enables one to concentrate on making a good corner joint. However, if the corner joint does not fit very snugly, all is not completely lost for the gap can, fairly successfully, be filled with a bead of white emulsion paint; with care this can be trimmed to a sharp enough corner with a craft knife and then touched up with paint. This technique, cribbed from Steven Clinch (a railway building modeller for Pendon), has succeeded in getting me out of trouble, but it is not a substitute for good folded corners.

Single brick string courses, often found on chimneys, can be made by gluing an overlay of embossed and painted card to the chimney. The position of this is better left unpainted, as the small quantities of glue used to secure such tiny items, takes to relatively unaltered card much better than to a well painted surface. In *Plate 47* there is a band (one brick wide, one brick course from the top) which only has the thin mortar colour on it for this reason.

The very common corbelled courses to be found towards the top of many chimneys can also be represented using strips of embossed

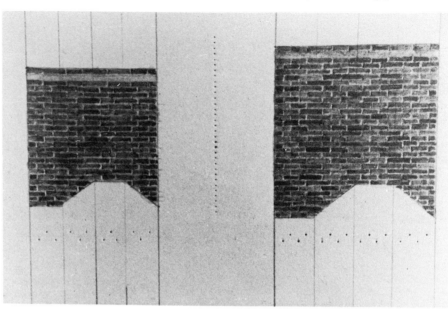

Plate 47a. Chimneys ready to be cut out and folded.

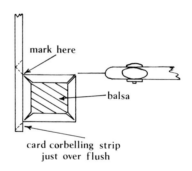

Fig. 46. Marking where to make a fold when wrapping strip card brick corbelling around a chimney.

and painted card. Before embossing and painting these, I make sure that each strip is cut to the correct length and has the vee cut-outs behind the corners in the right places. The position of the vees is determined by holding the card strip on one side of the chimney, with one end just projecting beyond an adjacent side and marking the distance with a craft knife held fairly tightly against the flat side of the chimney, as in *Fig. 46*.

With the strip back on the bench, I make the slight cut which marks the corner into a cut that penetrates the thickness of the card by approximately 75%. On either side of this cut I make angled cuts to produce a corner vee cut-out. With one folded corner made, I hold the strip to the chimney again and mark the next corner to be folded, repeating the procedure until the joint corner. Here I make a mitred joint which is made possible by ensuring that the ends project further than the corner by at least the thickness of the card

being used. After I have embossed and painted the strip with mortar colour, I glue it to the chimney, two sides at a time, and then paint the bricks.

For an alternative method that may be preferred — I seem to remember Penny Thompson ending her card tube beneath any upper corbelling and then gluing on steps of cut out 1 mm (brick depth) sheet, as in *Fig. 47*. I have also seen someone making the top few courses of three dimensional, individually cut, card bricks. This is quite a good method if the prototype requires the top bricks to appear to have lost the majority of their mortar. It also produces the correct thickness (if only one brick thickness) of brickwork when seen from above, as most models are. However, these two alternatives have the disadvantage that the vertical brick surface is based on what one might call the 'end grain' of the card. This can be tricky to paint, as the abnormal texture often tends to absorb the paint which appears darker than when applied to the normal surface which can make colour matching a problem.

The tops (plan view) of chimneys are very easy to make incorrectly, I'm sure I have done so on occasions. The internal dimensions can so often be wrongly assumed, because all we usually have to go on is the brick bond of the prototype viewed from ground level. I have seen photographs that show the tops of two or more chimneys (taken from higher buildings) where the bond and the overall size seemed to be the same but the visible thickness of the brickwork was 4½″ in one case and 9″ in another, (large flue, cheap job, small flue, expensive job?). Neither of

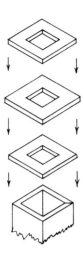

Fig. 47. Penny Thompson's method (I think) for representing the upper corbelling on a chimney.

Plate 47b.   *Roye England*

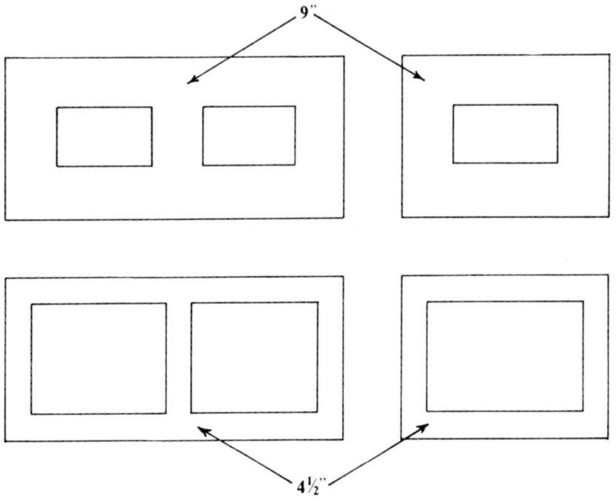

these, whether or not the bond was the same, can be represented satisfactorily with one thickness of 0.6 mm card, so to thicken up the card and bring it nearer to scale I have glued a strip of 1 mm card around the inside. For 9″ thickness I have cut a small insert (a variation on Penny Thompson's method), and glued that to the inside of the tube.

POTS

In some ways the easiest chimney top to deal with is one with a plain pot. Common round ones (with slight taper and lip at the top) have been turned from thinnish walled brass tube. 'Turned' sounds a little grand for my earlier ones, which were made with a wheel brace in the vice and a small selection of files. I make them 10 mm or so longer than they need be, part of the extra being glued into a hole bored in the balsa plug. I then fill the gap between the pot and card brickwork with Polyfilla, applied with a somewhat worn out paint brush. Several small applications may be necessary as there is some shrinkage involved. Conveniently, the vast majority of pots needed have been of the common type shown above, in different diameters and heights of course. For octagonal, square, fluted, louvred and other such fancy types, suitably fettled castings, of varying provenance, can be used.

The chimney projecting from one end of Willis' Cottage (see *Plate 47C*) had to be modelled with quite a severe curve in it. (Apparently this is often caused by sulphur finding its way into the brickwork and being expanded by the prevailing wind and rain. This can cause the stack to distort). At first I tried to bend a mock-up card tube for this

Fig. 48. By observation of some prototypes (from the top of a high tree), I can vouch for these four types of chimney top. There are, of course, many more.

Fig. 49. Section through a card tube chimney and turned brass pot. As a primer for the brass, I have, on different occasions, used matt white Humbrol and a mixture of very dilute PVA with just a little Polyfilla. Both these primers take water colour adequately and as the pots have not been subjected to much handling, the results are still satisfactory.

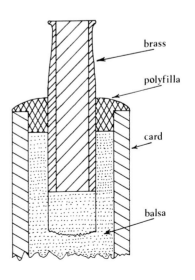

chimney but the assembly was remarkably rigid and did not want to take up the curve at all easily. The angles of the bricks on the surface development also needed some very fancy drawing so I gave up the idea of a curving card tube. Instead I carved a solid balsa chimney incorporating the curve. For the top I cut away (in little chips) a square hole some 5 mm deep, leaving a 1½ mm balsa wall, all round, and when painted black the bottom of the hole was hardly visible. After some sanding I had each surface square to its neighbour and flat enough to paint, although there was still some grain showing, so I gave the balsa a couple of coats of white emulsion. With rule and blunt knife I then grooved mortar lines and arrived at a reasonably close comparison with an embossed card surface which just took water colours acceptably. As emulsion is not particularly absorbent it was difficult not to leave little dots where I lifted the brush from the job when painting the bricks. In the wrong lighting a slight sheen was detectable that would not be acceptable on a larger area.

ROOF SUB BASES

As mentioned earlier, I glue a sheet of 0.2 mm card over the contoured roof profiles, or on a flat roof with straight profiles a thicker piece — 0.75 mm — so that unwanted contours are less likely to appear when gluing on tiles or slates. The card sheet may need to project over the eaves if a large overhang is necessary, otherwise the overhang of the actual tiles or slates is sufficient. I generally glue the card to the inside surfaces of the walls so that the roof card is flush with the eaves line. If there is a slight change in angle at the bottom of the roof, often the first two courses up from the

Plate 47c. A curving chimney on Willis' Cottage that needed quite a lot of thought.

Plate 48. The front of Canney Row with, on the left, what I shall call a 'Wiltshire type' and on the right an 'Oxfordshire type' of window.

gutter, the main side walls and roof profiles will have to incorporate the change and the roof card must be bent to suit. The roof card for thatched buildings is also made from 0.75 mm pasteboard but is seldom laid in one piece, as there are often windows to contend with.

I'm not sure that it is absolutely necessary, but, to be on the safe side, I have always made my card roofs for thatch follow the eventual shape — at least to a certain extent. I have a feeling it helps to ensure the desired result without putting on an extraordinary amount of hemp, only to later trim it away. With the 'Oxfordshire' type of window, the almost vertical bundles of straw on either side, must, in my opinion, have a near vertical surface on which to be glued.

Of course, there are other types to be seen — ridged dormers for instance. I have not had to represent this type yet, but looking at photographs of such prototypes there does not seem to be any need for special roof card structures.

Of course, the final shape of the thatch must largely be created at the trimming stage, but for half-hipped ends, such as the timbered end of the Leather Bottle Inn, I emulated the shape with the roof card, as in *Fig. 51.*

ROOF COVERINGS
THATCH
As I have just been writing about roof card for thatch, it seems logical to start this section with thatch. This is just as difficult to represent well, as slates and tiles, but it usually takes a fraction of the time. It is fairly well known that for many years Pendon thatch was made from Chinese human hair, but from the early 1970s plumbers hemp has been used. My method of thatching is based on that used by Rupert Godfrey on his Maiden Newton and Pendon models, although the ridge technique is my own.

The hemp (tow) that I have purchased has come in hanks approximately 2 ft long and 2 ins thick in the middle. From the hank I separate a smaller one of 2 ft by (when squeezed) about the thickness of a pencil.

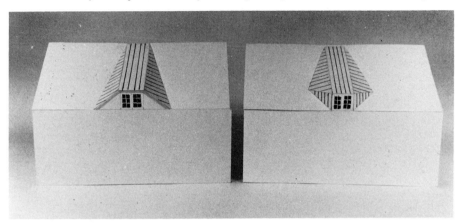

Plate 49. Two card mock-ups to illustrate the arrangement of card sub bases I make for 'Wiltshire type' (left) and 'Oxfordshire type' (right) windows. Both are quite common in Pendon's area. The trouble taken in making these window surrounds makes the final appearance of the thatch far more predictable.

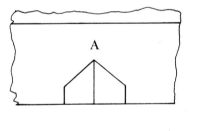 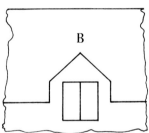 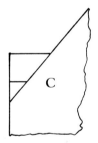

Fig. 50. Roof card arrangement for a 'common' ridged dormer window. A. plan, B. front elevation and C. end elevation.

   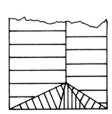

Fig. 51. The timbered end of The Leather Bottle Inn, where the eaves line end did not match the slope of the rest of the roof. By having three pieces of card following the shape of the somewhat rounded end, the fibres in the bundles of hemp are more likely to change direction gradually and therefore less obviously.

Working from the middle, I then pull the hank through my hands, alternately left and right, gently squeezing it between thumb and forefinger, until all the loose fibres have gathered at the ends; these are cut off and discarded. The small smooth hank is then cut into short bundles approximately 1 inch long (at this stage). In order to avoid the risk of destroying the uniformity of each bundle as it falls onto the bench I cut them over a box, to the side of which I can operate the scissors. There is nothing special about the scissors I use for this job but they are exceptionally sharp and are used for nothing but cutting hemp.

The bundles will be glued in courses all over the roof card, starting at the bottom, or, on a roof with a complicated eaves line, at the lowest point. I paint a band of neat PVA, between 5 and 10 mm wide and 2 or 3 ins long, along the roof card just above the eaves. A bundle is then dipped into a tray of PVA diluted 50/50. This will bond together the top ends of the hemp fibres, the bundle only being dipped into the mix by about 3 to 4 mm and wiped against the edge of the tray to leave the end of the bundle damp rather than soaking wet. The damp end is then placed on the glued band on the roof and pressed down into the neat glue. This process is repeated with more bundles, keeping each tight up to its neighbour and projecting downward from the eaves by approximately the remaining untreated 20 mm. I glue as many bundles as necessary to cover the 2 to 3 inches of glued card, then brush on some more for perhaps another 2 inches and continue applying the bundles to the first course.

When the end of the roof is reached, I push the glued ends of the bundles very tightly together (with a finger nail) as I glue them round the corner; this has the effect of fanning out each bundle slightly so that the fibres radiate from the glued area at diverging angles. I work the first course up the end a little, where the last bundle is at approximately 45°, as in *Fig. 52*.

It is very important that only just enough glue is used on the first two courses, both on the roof card and the tops of the bundles. If too much is used, it will gradually run down the fibres, too far below eaves level. This happened on parts of Canney Row and when I was ready to trim the eaves I found that the scissors were biting into a hard mass of hemp-reinforced PVA. I did manage, with great difficulty, to cut through the solid mass with a craft knife, but the strength required to grip the model really put the internal bracing to the test, and the force applied to the knife meant that when a piece finally gave way I

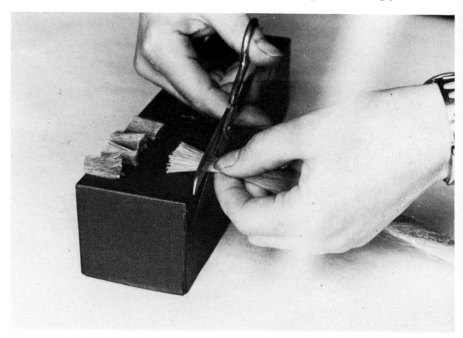

Plate 50. Cutting bundles of hemp, ready for thatching.

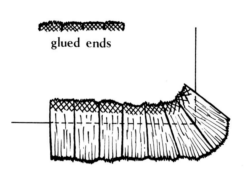

glued ends

Fig. 52. The first course of hemp bundles.

could not always stop the blade penetrating the card wall. As the cuts were under the eaves it was not a complete catastrophe, but since then I have not used so much glue on the first few courses!

I think all the thatched buildings I have seen in old photographs (modern practice is not relevant to this study) have had their eaves cut or shaped at 90° to the wall. To achieve this I hold the scissors at approximately 45° to the wall so that I cut the fibres nearest to the wall first. When the scissors bite into the hemp, the bundles are squashed, and cut in that attitude. If this precaution is not taken, when the bundle resumes its normal attitude some of the fibres can be shorter than desired (see. *Fig. 53*).

I do not attempt this operation in one go, but cut off a little at a time until I have the desired result. I use both straight and curved bladed scissors depending largely on how much I want to remove. I do not carry on

very far with the underside trimming before I also make a start on the main, sloping part of the roof, starting at the bottom. In fact, no one part of the trimming job is taken to completion in one stage, the character of the thatch is created, bit by bit, all over the roof, changing from one part to another.

If there is what I call a 'Wiltshire type' of window in the eaves line, I take the first course of hemp only a little way up its sloping sides. The direction of the fibres in each bundle, going over the window, is kept in line with those already laid on the main part of the roof. The rest of the dormer will be covered as successive courses take the thatch up the roof.

If, on the other hand, an 'Oxfordshire type' is required I glue a first course bundle on either side and then work away from it. This first bundle is approximately double normal thickness and is glued almost vertically on the specially made roof card. The thickness is double because this particular bundle will receive very little trimming and must project from the roof card as much as the normal sloping bundles that will be glued against it. Only the very end of this first bundle is dipped into the tray of dilute PVA as the bundles glued above will only just cover its top; glue matted hemp does not look at all straw-like, so I take great care to ensure that none will be visible on the finished model.

On large ridged dormer types the straw usually abuts the side wall of the dormer, and that is where I would make my start. The tops of such dormers are, in the real thing, often treated as a separate little roof. I think I

Plate 51. The mock-up of the 'Wiltshire type' window with the first course of hemp bundles glued in place. Also in the photograph are a container of Evo-Stik Resin W PVA, a tray of dilute PVA, a jar to hang the glue brush in water, and some ready-cut hemp bundles.

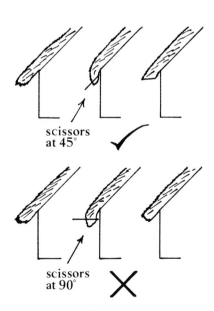

scissors
at 45°

scissors
at 90°

Fig. 53. To make 90° eaves, the large first bites with the scissors are, strangely, made with the scissors at 45° to the wall.

Plate 52. The mock-up of the 'Oxfordshire type' window, with the first, almost vertical bundle, and a second, beginning the transition to slope back. When hard, the projecting fibres can be trimmed above the vertical piece or roof card.

Plate 53a. An early 1930s photograph of a pair of chalkstone, brick and thatch cottages in the village of Bishopstone, Wiltshire. How well kept the grass is.
                                                                                                 Roye England

Plate 53b. A street in Bishopstone, Wiltshire. The eaves line on this row of cottages really intrigues me, obviously not architect-designed, and very appealing in modelling terms.
                                                                                                 Roye England

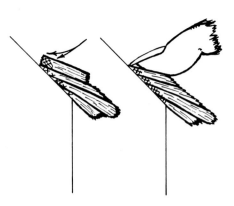

Fig. 54.

Plate 54. The 'Oxfordshire type' mock-up with three courses glued in place.

would completely thatch the main roof, trim it and ridge it before starting on the dormer roof. However, if in the prototype it appeared integral with the main roof, then it would be treated at the same time.

Having dealt with the first course, bundles for the second are cut about 1⅛″ long to overlap the first ones at the top and bottom. This time I brush the 5-10 mm band of glue just on and above the top ends of the first course. The extra long bundles are then dipped and glued over the first course. This extra long second course ensures a thick covering at the eaves. For the third course I revert to 1″ bundles and then slightly shorter ones for the rest of the roof. The third and upper courses are glued in place initially directly over and in line with the previous course. However, the fibres of these bundles are graded to the slope of the roof by gently prodding the fibres up the roof into the wet glue as in *Fig. 54*.

This technique of having the ends of the bundles at a similar angle to the slope of the roof, and top surfaces almost horizontal, requires less trimming and not so much of the fibres sides are visible. The type of thatch can be suggested by varying the angle of the bundles of hemp. If the bundles are laid with their top surfaces sloping at a similar angle to the roof, a very 'long straw' effect could result when trimmed. In fact, the hemp fibres visible would be longer than the scale of real 'long straw' thatching. The nearer the hemp bundles are laid to horizontal, the more the eventual thatch surface will be made of just the fibre ends. This is desirable perhaps if representing a 'combed wheat reed' type of thatch. This texture, though, is difficult to achieve towards the ridge, so I compromise

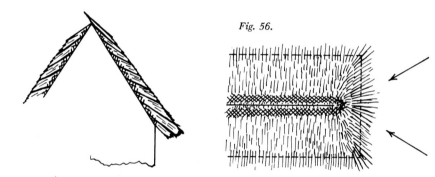

Fig. 56.

Fig. 55. The angle of the bundles changing towards the top and the dipped ends of the top course projecting above the ridge.

Plate 55. Some of the glued ends of the top course of bundles are projecting above the roof. To speed up the setting process, so that I can cut these ends off fairly promptly, I place the model quite close under a bench lamp. When the glued fibres have become quite a dark colour, the cutting off can be attempted. I don't wait until the glue has gone rock hard as that makes the ridge modelling very frustrating, as explained later. When one side has been cut off, the top course on the other side can be glued on, projecting in the same way. On a gable end these two top courses fan out at the end of the ridge to make a complete covering, as in Fig. 56. This does not apply at the top of hipped ends as the hemp has been worked around the end anyway, as in Plate 56.

Plate 56a. A timber-built (card and balsa) byre, with the courses of hemp nearing the ridge; the next courses will be angled more nearly to the slope of the roof. As can be seen, the bundles of hemp fan out around the hipped end.   *A. E. Smith*

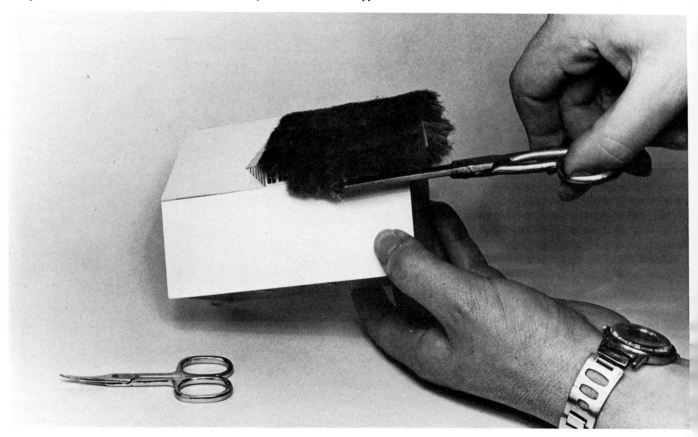

Plate 56b. Trimming the eaves with the scissors held at 45° to the wall; this will produce a 90° angle between the eaves and the wall.

Plate 57a. Tony Smith, helping out as ever, measuring the overhang of thatch at Holborn Farm, Letcombe Basset. As the farm is built on chalk, there is presumably no drainage problem in the hollow where Tony is standing. *Roye England*

and usually make a short sort of 'long straw-cum-long reed' type by having the bundles fairly near to horizontal.

Towards the top of the roof I make the bundles progressively shorter and lay them at increasingly steeper angles, from nearly horizontal to midway between the slope of the roof and horizontal (see Fig. 55). When I reach the top of the roof card, I grade the top course so that some of the dipped ends project above the roof. When hard, these ends are cut off level with the card ridge, with a craft knife. However, if I have reached the stage shown in Plate 56 at the end of an evening or at some other time when it would be impossible to continue, the final few courses should not be laid. The trimming operation over most of the roof might best be carried out before tackling the ridge area.

When trimming the main part of the roof, or a gable or hipped end, the scissors are held so that they are cutting against the direction of the fibres (see *Plate 58a*) up the roof, on the main part, and at 45° or so at the corner bundles, when trimming them. The more densely the bundles have been laid, the more difficult it is to trim them. It is very easy to produce a 'ridge and furrow' surface if large bites are taken with the scissors. So the more dense the thatch, the longer the trimming will take, as only small bites with the scissors are made. I have tried safety razors, but they have practically no effect. Electric razors just agitate the fibres rather than cut them.

Plate 57b. It looks as though we are looking up a back alley with a slight feeling of industrial back-to-back rows, but I am pretty sure that the door on the right is, or was, a front door. I wonder why the window near the door was blocked up? What appears to be a brick pathway may be just that, but I am fairly sure that, being slightly hollowed, it doubled as a drain and probably not just for the water that fell from the enormous overhang of the thatch. The two large stones in the foreground bridge a small stream into which the water etc. would fall. *Roye England*

In the Vale of White Horse the thatch at gable ends often overhung the wall by up to 2 ft and finished at a sharpish edge. Another method I have seen is apparent in 1950s photographs of the Leather Bottle Inn where the thatch was bound and pegged back in a long sort of bundle at the gable, only just projecting from the wall. I do not expect this was necessarily a 1950s method, but perhaps, more likely, the style chosen by the particular thatcher. Earlier and later photographs show the same building with what I have found to be the more normal, 'sharpish edge', type. The 'bound and pegged' type does not seem to be peculiar to any area, as I have also seen it in the Kettering area.

As the earlier photographs of the Leather Bottle showed the more normal type of gable treatment, I did not model the 'bound and pegged' method, but if I had, at the corner I would have angled the bundles at around 25° instead of the normal 45°. With not so much projecting, the overhanging bundles would only need a little trimming just to neaten them up, and to make the flat-ended look. I would then have pegged them back towards the wall using my normal pegging materials, which I will come to shortly.

After I have trimmed the whole roof I tackle the ridge. My ridging technique calls for a set, but not rock hard, area of glue-matted hemp at the top of the roof. Because this is critical, the ridge area is not tackled until I can guarantee an uninterrupted period sufficient to do the whole job. To complete the ridge area of the byre shown in *Plate 56* would take me almost a whole day. When the projecting fibres have been trimmed from one side of the roof, the projecting bundles for the other side can be laid. When set, the final projections can be cut off and the ridge area bundles trimmed to blend with the rest of the roof. As mentioned earlier, I try to avoid having any glue-matted hemp visible and for this reason I do not use any glue at all in securing the ridge bundles. First, I cut each bundle just long enough to cover the ridge from half-way up each top course, as in *Fig. 58*.

I usually halve the pencil thickness for ridge bundles so they can easily be bent in the middle to fit the ridge. Inverted V-shaped bundles are placed closely side by side along the ridge and held down to the roof with khaki-coloured cotton and little staples made from steel wire (Plate 61a).

I drape a line of cotton over the somewhat untidy looking ridge bundles, then with a staple (peg) in the pliers I fix the cotton in place. If there are to be two lines of thread, I

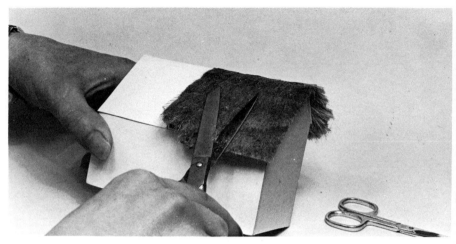

Plate 58a. Trimming the main part of the roof.

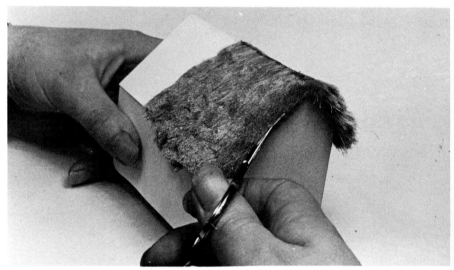

Plate 58b. Here I have rounded off the top surface leading to the 'sharpish edge' and am now making the undercut for the other side of the pointed overhang, so often seen in the Vale. Again I am using one of the thatching mock-ups.

Plate 59. The quick 'Oxfordshire type' mock-up, now with the window area trimmed. On a real model, I take great care not to damage any of the glazing bars with stray scissors. Mended ones never look as good. To prevent this happening and to stop trimmed fibres falling into any open windows, I cover the whole window with a piece of scrap card before trimming.

Plate 60. What first struck me about this picture was the lack of chimneys, but as it is actually two cottages joined together, the original heating arrangements must have been altered to suit the new layout.

Roye England

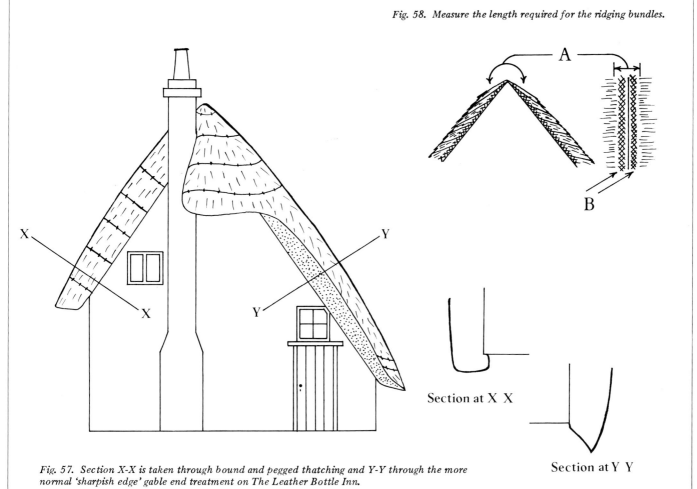

Fig. 58. Measure the length required for the ridging bundles.

Section at X X

Section at Y Y

Fig. 57. Section X-X is taken through bound and pegged thatching and Y-Y through the more normal 'sharpish edge' gable end treatment on The Leather Bottle Inn.

usually start with the top one. The little staples are gripped with pliers rather than tweezers as they are pushed through the half hard glue of the top courses of bundles that the ridge partly covers. Even when just half hard (having only had something like 2 or 3 hours to set) the staples need a very firm push to penetrate the glue. If left for much longer the glue sets with such a hard skin that the staples are not strong enough to penetrate. On one occasion I had to throw away virtually every other staple, having bent them irrevocably, trying to push them into place.

I space the pegs at approximately 10 mm intervals along one side and then, with another or a continuation of the same piece of cotton, I do the same on the other side. If I have pegged the cotton down in an unacceptable line or wandered off from parallel with the ridge, the staples can be removed and repositioned. After a satisfactory line has been achieved more pegs are pushed in between each 10 mm gap, so making 5 mm spacings. In order to flatten the bundles of hemp in between the pegs, the cotton is pulled taut from time to time. I try not to thrust the pegs in too far as this can lead to a wavy ridge, but just far enough to hold the hemp flat. If an undesirable line appears, the ridge can be blended to the rest of the roof with a little trimming.

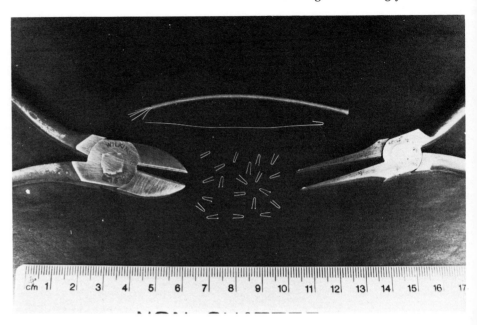

Plate 61a. At the top is the stranded cable I use for thatching pegs. Beneath is one strand (the end of which I have bent in the pliers) waiting to be cut off. In the middle are finished staples ready to be used.

Other pegs and runners, as I call them, appear on most thatched roofs, around hipped ends and just a little way in from the eaves, for instance. For these I lay the cotton on the roof but if the glue-matted hemp is either too deep below the surface or at the eaves overhang or not there at all, I glue the pegs in position. Before putting each peg in place, I dip it into some PVA, holding it in tweezers this time, as no force is required. Each dipped peg is then gently eased into the thatch until it secures the cotton.

Plate 61b. Pegging down the ridge bundles with little steel wire staples and khaki coloured cotton.

Plate 62. The many pegs and runners in use here may well be holding down fairly new repairs necessitated by the gregarious nesting nature of the common house sparrow.
Roye England

Fortunately, raised ornamental ridges, commonly seen on thatched roofs today, were virtually non-existent in Pendon's area during the 1920s and 30s and so I have not had to tackle them! Ornamentation with the pegs and runners though was quite common, especially in a 'criss-crossed' form, as in *Plate 64.*

For these I have pegged two parallel threads of cotton along the thatch. Then, at the prototype's spacing, I have pegged another length of cotton at opposite angles up and down between the parallel ones, as in *Fig. 59.*

Plate 63. A fairly quick mock-up of a fully pegged ridge, just to give the general idea.

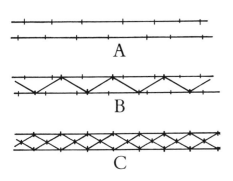

Fig. 59. A. shows the first stage, two parallel runs of pegs and runners holding the ridge bundles down. B. The second stage, a length of cotton pegged at diagonals. C. The final stage, another piece of cotton pegged across the second stage piece, in order to make the series of crosses and diamonds. The pegs that held the first two parallel runs (A) would be pulled out and repositioned to hold the diagonal runs.

Plate 64. Thatched barn from the village of Denchworth, with ornamental crossed runners.

Plate 65a. More evidence of sparrows in the roof of this gorgeous barn. Presumably there was a problem with valleys in the thatch, hence the tiled area around the doorway roof. To the right of the gates is a heap of free-range piglets, not a common sight these days. *Roye England*

Plate 65b. What a lovely rounded shape this roof has, not easy to model but a very common feature of period thatch. The bulge in the wall, with its little roof, may well have something to do with an oven of some sort. Again only upstairs windows are open. *Roye England*

The patching of thatch is quite common where small areas have become less weather-proof than desirable. Copying photographs of the prototype, the patches shown in *Plate 66a*, were made by trimming a gully in the hemp, which was then filled with quite thin, fresh bundles. These additional bundles were laid in such a way that their fibres were lying at a different angle to the main roof fibres, still running up and down the roof but more nearly similar to the pitch of the roof. This difference in fibre angle did not seem very logical but was visible in the photographs of the real thing. The patches also seemed to be proud of the main roof by a few inches.

Although the projection and different fibre angles on the model made the patches fairly noticeable, they can be accentuated by painting them a slightly paler colour than the main part, so that they don't appear so old and weathered.

If the prototype demands a thatch in good condition, then of course I strive for an equally good model thatch; if on the other hand a dilapidated thatch is called for, a different approach is necessary.

As *Plate 66b* shows, some of the thatch has fallen away completely to show timbering. This was modelled before thatching began, using balsa wood and card strips. Old thatch can have a sad, droopy, look about it and it is often considerably thinner than when new. For this reason far less hemp is put on the roof, not just thinner bundles, but thinned by pushing them up the slope further when grading them to the roof's pitch, making them go further and lie at a steeper angle than on a roof in good condition.

When trimming such a roof, gullies in the main part and the tattiness of the eaves are created with the scissors. Ridge bundles are pegged in place in the conventional way, but perhaps not so neatly; similarly, any other pegs and runners.

When painting dilapidated thatch, I have used a variety of thinned matt Humbrol colours, brushed on in patches. The colours, based on my observation of such roofs, range from an almost black green for a very damp shaded roof, through pale buffish brown, for old but unweathered straw, where thatch has recently fallen out, to an almost silver grey where the thatch is very dry and sun bleached. Sometimes, pale and quite bright moss colour is added afterwards for a thin covering of such growths, on a fairly sunny side. On a shaded side the mosses can be quite luxuriant and need to be represented by more than just a coat of paint (see page 74). Small

Plate 66a. Patched up thatch at the back of Canney Row.

Plate 66b. A roadside field building from Challow that has been somewhat neglected.

round holes made by birds that live or work in the thatch can be made with the point of a scriber after the paint has dried.

When painting thatch in reasonably good condition, I have again used matt Humbrols but not in quite such a variety of colours as with a dilapidated one. My first thatched building was painted with a very thin mix of matt earth and matt black; to my horror I found the thinners soaking through the hemp and into the timber cladding on the walls, this did not happen immediately but some little

while after I had painted the whole roof, so there was practically nothing I could do about it. Fortunately all that happened was that the water colour card planks became darker in colour and had a slight sheen. It's a good job the walls were not brick or stone. Subsequently I used considerably less thinners but this was still less than ideal as the paint matted the hemp fibres together.

For my third thatched model I made a scrap card masking box around the walls, etc, and sprayed the colour onto the roof. The

Plate 66c. Huge areas of thatch like this would look just as impressive if modelled, but in 4mm scale a building of this size might well be two feet long. The two thatched brick outshots on either side of the door may well be evidence of increased prosperity at some stage whereas the corrugated iron one may reflect leaner times. The wall to its right seems to be brick-framed with rough hewn stone infill.   *Roye England*

masking box for a house is very often a more complicated structure than for a barn, for instance, because of windows that are often in the eaves. Little box tube masks are also required for chimneys. The effort of making these masks is to me worthwhile, as sprayed (just a little thinned) paint does not destroy the delicate texture created by the hemp fibres.

The colour of thatch varies, of course, depending amongst other things, on how old it is. Very neat, consistently textured model thatch is extremely difficult (if not impossible) to represent, so I do not attempt brand new thatch and haven't needed new straw colour.

Other Pendon modellers have represented two year old thatch with Humbrol Matt Dark Earth, but I am not very keen on this as I think it is too plain and dull, and, if anything, too brown. I favour the colour of, say, fifteen year old thatch, which in many cases seems to be a 'charcoaly' sort of grey between the straws, although their outer ends seem to be much paler, more like the dry, sun-bleached silver grey I mentioned earlier. On some of the thatched buildings I have pretty well achieved this effect with one dark grey coat of paint, sprayed into the hemp, and another, pale grey mix, just lightly sprayed over the top.

Plate 66d. The same huge barn but viewed from the other end. Although the thatch is a little 'moth-eaten', the overall impression is of a very smooth surfaced thatch, not at all easy to reproduce. To have any hope of a faithful representation, the bundles of hemp would need to be laid very densely which makes the roof difficult to trim, as little scallop marks can easily be left by the scissors.   *Roye England*

Plate 67. The Old Vicarage with its roof of small clay tiles.

TILES

The vast majority of tiles in Pendon's area and period were small hand-made clay tiles about ⅝″ thick, with a visible area around 4″ to 5″ deep and 6″ wide, slightly raised in the centre so that water ran off the curved surface easily. These can be represented using medium weight cartridge paper ruled with a grid of pencil lines and cut with scissors and knife. I find this marking out a very laborious task which often turns out unsatisfactorily, for 100% accuracy of line spacings is to me virtually unattainable.

I have recently had access to a photocopier and run the cartridge paper through the machine, printing a facsimile of 1 mm graph paper onto it. As the cartridge paper is somewhat thicker than the copying paper the toner does not take all that well, just adequately.

With a small pair of sharp scissors I make a cut every 2 mm along a sheet, approx 2 mm into it, and then cut (with craft knife and straight edge) a 5 mm wide strip from the sheet.

After cutting sufficient strips to cover the roof, Roye would paint the tiles individually and then glue each strip in place. I have not

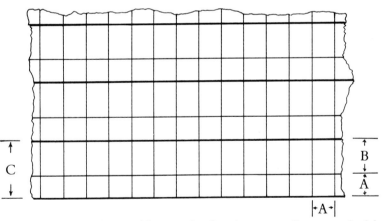

Fig. 60. Pencil line grid marked on cartridge paper for tile strips — a very time-consuming job. A = 2mm exposed area. B = 3mm overlap. C = eventual strip 5mm high.

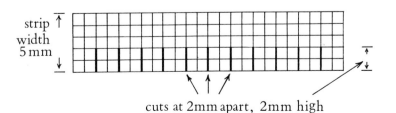

cuts at 2mm apart, 2mm high

Fig. 61. A strip of cartridge paper with the impression of 1mm graph paper photo-copied onto it, and scissor cuts made. With hand-ruled paper, the scissor cutting operation can compound any pencilled inaccuracies and make satisfactory gap offsetting a major problem.

Plate 68. The Old Vicarage with quite a number of plain white paper strip, scissor-cut tiles glued in place. The change of angle at the right-hand side, from an east-west to a north-south roof, is worth consideration. This model would, in the main, be viewed in the same direction as the photograph was taken. To avoid unsightly gaps at the corner being visible (100% accurate fitting tiles at such a corner are unlikely), I have carried the east-west tiles right into the corner. The north-south tiles will then butt up against these, so making any gaps far less noticeable, as in Fig. 62.

the experience, or confidence in the end result, to do that, so I glue the strips of tiles to the roof card before painting.

At appropriate spacings up the roof card I mark pencil guide lines to assist spacing and to help keep the courses of tiles horizontal. For a roof in good condition, strips the full length of the roof are glued in place, but for one that has seen better days, I cut the odd corner off various tiles and glue differing lengths of strips in place, sometimes fifteen to twenty on one strip, four or five, and the occasional individual one, especially if one is meant to have slipped a little. At the bottom of a roof there are usually two courses laid virtually one upon the other so that there are no uncovered gaps above the wall.

I glue the tile strips in place by brushing a band of PVA along the roof card and the 3 mm overlap area (or, maybe it should be underlap area) and placing the strip, photocopier ink downwards, onto the wet glue. I then rub the back of a finger nail along the strip to ensure a good fixture. Any glue that oozes from beneath the tiles I scrape away with a craft knife, as the water colour that will be applied does not take to PVA very well.

At the ridge the overlap parts of the strips project beyond the top of the roof when the

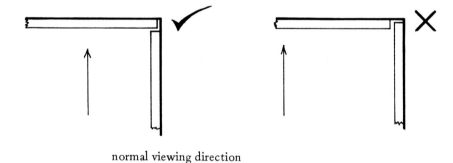

normal viewing direction

Fig. 62.

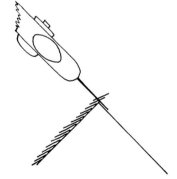

Fig. 63. At the ridge the overlap parts of the strips project beyond the top of the roof when the actual tiles are glued in place. When set, the projecting paper is trimmed away with a knife.

actual tiles are glued in place. When set, the projecting paper is trimmed away with a knife.

PANTILES

Although I have not had to represent pantiles, I have noticed them in old photographs of the Vale, so I carried out a small experiment to test a theory of how they could be represented. The type I have modelled has a large concave curve leading to a sharper radius, convex overlap, as in *Fig. 64.*

On the mock roof card I glued lengths of approx 22 gauge tinned copper wire stripped from electrical cable and pulled taut to straighten them. These were glued at 1/10″ spacings. I then marked out a piece of cartridge paper from which to cut individual tiles. The measurements I used were a bit of a mixture of units, but they suited the prototype sizes as shown in *Fig. 65.*

Each 5 mm × ⅛″ tile cut from the sheet then had two diagonally opposite corners cut off so they would lie correctly on the roof. To bend the flat pieces of paper into the tile shape *(Fig. 65b)* I gripped area *A* of the paper with tweezers so that area *B* projected from the side. I then bent the paper against the tweezers to make the sharp radius overlap curve. With the bent paper still held in the tweezers, I made the large radius curve (other half of the S bend) using my thumb nail.

I laid them individually starting at the bottom right hand corner of the mock-up, applying a blob of glue sufficient to nearly half fill the space between a pair of wires where one tile would be placed, and so on.

I think the biggest problem with the technique is judging the correct amount to cut from the corners — not enough and the tile won't sit in its place correctly, too much and a gap shows, as can be seen on my experiment. However, when painted, the little gaps were not easily detectable, and so I think the technique is reasonably satisfactory for small lean-to outbuildings and the like. A large country house, on the other hand, would be extremely tedious to cover in this way.

Plate 69. An experiment to test a theory of how pantiles could be modelled.

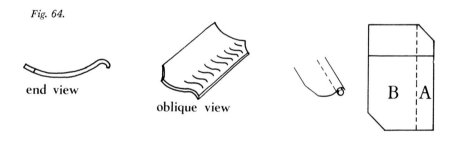

Fig. 64.

end view

oblique view

B   A

Fig. 65b. Individual pantile with corners cut.

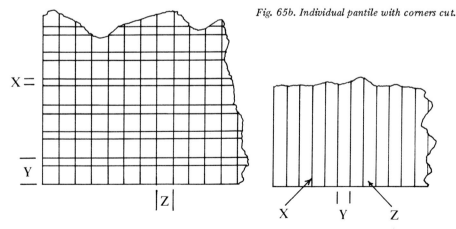

X =

Y

|Z|

X   Y   Z

Fig. 65a. Marked out cartridge paper for pantiles.

X = 1½mm
Y = 5mm
Z = ⅛ inch

Fig. 65c.   X = approx. 22 swg wire
Y = ¹⁄₁₀″ wire spacing
Z = roof card

Plate 70. Strips of paper have been cut and glued in place on the roof card and then painted with a thin wash of water colour. This acts as an undercoat and should ensure that all the edges of the tiles are coloured. The tiny little pale patches, less than the size of a tile, have not been missed when painting but are the result of glue getting on the exposed area of the paper strips and not being scraped away sufficiently. The somewhat thicker mix used when painting each tile should, with care, cover these patches.

Plate 71. About half an hour's application of the first mix of tile colour, dotted around at random. As can be seen, some of the tiles appear considerably darker than others. The reason for this desirable variation in tone is that although the paint is of the same mix, taken from the same area of the palette, the first few tiles, painted with a freshly loaded brush, come out darker, as the paint is more dense — so each tile gets progressively paler before more paint is required.

Plate 72. The same roof but now with another random application of a slightly different mix, with perhaps one of the three basic constituents being changed, i.e. Burnt Umber, Cadmium Scarlet and a touch of Charcoal Grey instead of Light Red, Cadmium Scarlet and a touch of Charcoal Grey.

Plate 73. A further random application of paint to individual tiles with yet another mix — possibly Burnt Sienna, a little Light Red and even less Charcoal Grey. At this stage the final appearance is easier to envisage and the last blend to choose becomes more obvious. It could be one of the previous mixes or a completely new one if, say, a richer red or a paler, more brown colour is thought to be desirable to finish off with.

PAINTING TILES

When the strips of tiles have been fixed to the roof card and trimmed off at ridges and gables, the painting begins. It may seem easier to paint them before they are glued in place, but I found it difficult to judge and attain the correct colour.

My test piece for Pendon, a small lock keeper's hut, had to have a slate roof (the basic painting principles are the same for both slates and tiles). As recommended, these slates, made from cut paper strips, were painted before being glued in place. However, because PVA does not always take to water colour painted surfaces all that well, each strip was only painted on the area that would eventually be exposed, the overlap portion of each slate being left as bare paper. The staring white of the bare overlap portion so confused my judgement regarding the final appearance that I had very little confidence in my blends of colour. Therefore, after painting only half a dozen or so, I decided to glue the unpainted paper strips onto the roof card and then give the whole roof a thin wash with a medium tone of my chosen colours. I found this much better as there was no longer any staring white paper to confuse my judgement of how the job was going.

I have used the above procedure for all roofs covered with cut paper strips, overcoming the difficulties of access to awkward areas by building a stack of books, tins and the like, on which to support my painting hand.

The series of photographs opposite were taken during the painting of one section of the Old Vicarage to show tile painting. They start with the thin medium tone wash and follow through the individual painting of each tile, to the stage where the completed roof just needs ridge tiles and weathering.

The colours used for tiles are usually very similar to those used when painting bricks, i.e. Light Red, Cadmium Scarlet, Burnt Umber, Burnt Sienna, Cadmium Orange with possibly a touch of Brown Madder, Charcoal Grey and Chinese White. I would not normally use all these colours in one mix, but combinations of three or four depending on the shade of reddish brown required. An overall greenish appearance is very often required on the finished model but this effect is best created at the weathering stage.

Plate 74. All the tiles have now been individually painted with varying densities of three or four subtly differing mixes of water colour. Now, only the ridge tiles and some weathering, i.e. lichens, mosses and the like, remain to be done.

Asbestos Tiles

Although I have not had to model asbestos tiles, they cannot be ignored as they are not uncommon, especially on 1920s and 30s bungalows. They also had a profound influence upon Roye. During his early days in England (at the village of Wanborough to the east of Swindon) he witnessed the stripping of thatch from an old pub, and was horrified to find it being replaced by pink asbestos tiles which, in his opinion, ruined what was once a very attractive building that had blended so well with its surroundings. It was the very disappearance of such rural harmony that led to Roye's desire to record some of the unspoilt Vale in model form, which fifty years later we know as Pendon.

When one of Pendon's modellers, Peter Gentle, had to tackle asbestos tiles, we had quite a long discussion about possible techniques. He eventually decided that the way to do it was to cut and glue on individual tiles, and thankfully the roof was not very big.

Strips perhaps could have been used but precise consistency in manufacture would have been difficult.

At the survey stage it was ascertained that the angle at the bottom point of each tile was 105° and so the visible area of each tile was not a square as previously supposed.

Starting at the eaves, Peter glued a 5 mm strip of paper to the roof card on which to lay the first course of full tiles. The remaining courses were laid so as to cover the joins between the tiles in each lower course. Peter made suitable colour mixes using Light Red, Brown Madder, Chinese White & Charcoal Grey.

Ridge Tiles

I make half-round clay ridge tiles using small, tile-sized (often 4 mm long by 3 ½ mm wide), pieces of paper that I have curved around a piece of wire. On occasions, these have been painted before gluing into place, but this has not been a strict rule.

I make sharp-angled blue ridge tiles in the same way but obviously with a sharp bend. A common variation of this type has a cylindrical projection or 'roll' along the top. This can be represented by gluing a piece of wire along the ridge, and wrapping very thin paper tiles over the top, following the shape of the wire, as in *Fig. 67*.

For particularly ornate ridge tiles (often found on station buildings), I would either cut a strip of paper to shape, or use a commercial etching if a suitable one was available.

Plate 75a. A small pre-Second War bungalow with asbestos roof tiles. The model was made for Pendon by Peter Gentle, who normally works in 3mm scale.

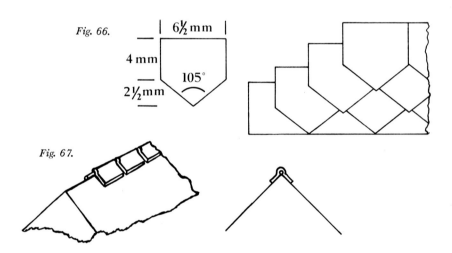

Fig. 66.

6½ mm

4 mm

2½ mm

105°

Fig. 67.

Plate 75b.

Slates ("Welsh type")

By 'Welsh type' I mean thin blue/grey varieties which may in fact have come from Cumbria, or somewhere other than Wales. They came in various sizes with names such as Duchess and Countess; I cannot quote actual sizes but I know the visible portion ranged from about 2 ft to some 9 ins. The sizes used on a model can be determined either by measuring the exposed area on site, or by calculation, i.e. dividing the number in their courses over a known distance.

To begin with I mark out a piece of suitably thin paper (Silvine writing paper), with lines defining the exposed areas and overlap areas of slate strips, as in *Fig. 68*.

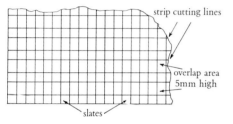

Fig. 68. Thin writing paper marked out for slates.

Then working from the bottom of the marked out sheet, I next produce the necessary individual appearance of each slate before cutting the sheet into strips, after all a sheet of paper, slowly decreasing in size is far easier to handle than a strip possibly only 8 mm wide. Although with tiles I cut the vertical line dividing each one from the next with scissors, when making slates I actually remove a small piece of paper from between the slates with a knife, as in *Fig. 69*.

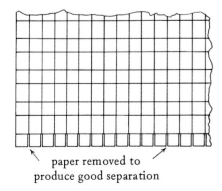

Fig. 69. Thin writing paper, cut to represent slates.

Plate 76. A long slate roof covering two adjacent lean-to extensions of Wharf Cottage.

A. E. Smith

Plate 77a. This old implement shed seems now to be the resting place for unused vehicles, the likes of which have thankfully been restored by many people, although the forlorn appearance of such scenes has its appeal. The main reason for including this picture is to show the mosses and lichens on the slates. The building has not suffered complete neglect, though, as some replacement slates have been fitted at the eaves. The little strips of metal that hold them in place would be very fiddly to make.

Roye England

With a new blade in the knife handle, I make an incision on either side of the slate dividing lines, working along the full length of one row. Then with the 'rough jobs knife' held upside down (the very tip of its blade broken off) I tear away each little piece of paper from between the incisions, their small attachment to the overlap portion is easily broken sufficiently cleanly. The reason for creating a gap is that as slate paper is considerably thinner than tile paper and is painted with a thicker mix than tiles, a single scissor cut would be very easy to lose altogether.

Having removed all the little bits of paper from one row of slates I then cut the full strip (including the overlap area) from the sheet.

Before gluing the strips in place, some guide lines can be drawn on the roof card to assist parallel application. I apply glue to the roof card with an old paint brush, making sure that the glue will fix both the slate and overlap areas of each strip. Starting with the first strip overhanging the eaves, the second strip is then glued almost directly upon the first, so that there are no gaps above the wall, (prototype practice usually) apparent in *Plate 32* on page 28. The strips should, of course, overhang gable ends by at least half a slate and possibly one and a half if projecting barge boards are to be fitted.

After fixing a strip in place I check to see if any glue has oozed out on to an exposed surface, and scrape it away. In order that any glue in the little gaps will not be a problem

later on when painting, I scrub it lightly with a thin slate colour loaded brush so as to dilute and colour the glue at the same time. Any trace of glue should then be easily covered at the main, individual slate-painting stage.

When the ridge is reached I do not worry if I have not finished with exactly a whole slate's depth to be visible beneath the ridge tiles, as on real roofs some rather odd adjustments are quite often made there, sometimes with less than half a slate visible and other times, just over half a slate laid on its side. The overlap portions of the last few courses that project above the roof card ridge are cut off when the glue has set, likewise any trimming that may be necessary at gable ends.

When working into corners with slates, I use the same principle as described for tiles (see page 58).

Painting ("Welsh type") Slates
When the roof has been completely covered with paper slates and the glue has had time to set, I wash the whole roof over with a thin medium-toned slate colour mix. This undercoat makes sure that all the slates edges are coloured and removes the glaring white of the paper.

As mentioned earlier, a thicker than normal mix is used for the individual painting of slates. The reason is that slates are usually considerably larger than tiles or bricks and normally require a more even and darker covering of colour. Very small patches of a thinly covered tile, showing a paler tone than

other parts of the same tile, do not seem to matter and may be important enough to contribute to the final appearance, but the sort of tiles I deal with are themselves quite small. An unevenly covered slate, on the other hand, does not look at all convincing to me. The size of the slates may make the problem more apparent, but I also think that the more noticeable contrast between a well covered area and a not so well covered area of a slate is because fairly dark colours are involved. So although the white of card or paper showing through the paint is sometimes a great advantage, with slates it is certainly not. Real slates that I have come across have a remarkably dense and uniform appearance and to that end I like the paint mix to be capable of covering in one coat. It is difficult to describe the consistency, but perhaps something midway between that of plain water and undiluted/fresh white PVA would be somewhere near. If artists water colours are applied any more thickly, there is a possibility of the surface crazing in quite a short time, given the wrong conditions, i.e. too hot and dry.

The basic colours I use are Davy's Grey, Brown Madder, Viridian Green and Chinese White. If a blue-grey is required and I cannot achieve the correct colour using the above, a small quantity of Payne's Grey is added. The Davy's Grey is by far the main constituent of any slate mix (I believe its pigment has ground slate in it). Viridian Green is used sparingly as it is quite a powerful colour, and

Plate 77b. This group from Sparsholt amply shows the wide variety of building materials used in the 'Vale', stonework, rendering and timber walls and, as we are in the roofs section, thatch, slate, small 'flat tiles', corrugated tiles and pantiles. It is interesting that the sagging roof of the centre building is wavy in the tiled portion and an even sag in the slate section. Maybe the latter is an outshot from an earlier tiled building.   *Roye England*

the Brown Madder and Chinese White proportions are increased if a more purple colour is required. For some kinds, possibly a touch of Charcoal Grey could be beneficial.

Limestone Slates
As the name suggests, roofs covered with this type of slate are usually only found in and around an area where the necessary form of limestone is available. In the Stamford area they are known as Collywestern slates, in Sussex and Surrey as Horsham slates, and in the Cotswolds and the 'Vale' they are known as Stonesfield slates. Apart from the usual size reduction as the courses get nearer to the ridge, they are noted for the amount of mosses and lichens that attach themselves, especially on the normally shaded and consequently damp side. Presumably, the individual and all-over rough texture of the slates and roof encourage the attachment of the plants. This texture can be represented by artists' water colour paper (Whatman and the like) or chemists' filter paper — both have proved very suitable.

The size of these slates varies, and it is necessary to at least establish the size used in the first course, and better still, some of the sizes at various points higher up the roof. Apparently the real slaters have names for the different sized courses.

Because of the variation, I do not lay out a large sheet of paper with cutting lines, but instead, mark each course separately, allowing for a 4 mm overlap area, plus the visible depth of the first course of slates. If

possible I prefer each strip to be long enough to overhang the eaves at either end, but this is not necessary if, as is often the case, the end walls of the building project above the roof line. The vertical cutting lines that correspond to the gaps between the slates are marked along each strip, then, as with 'Welsh type' slates, I make a cut on either side of these lines and remove a small piece of paper. As limestone slates are far less mechanical-looking and appear to have slightly rounded

corners, I also make a series of cuts at the corners and bottom edges to give this effect, as I hope is apparent in *Plate 78*.

The strip is then cut from the sheet and glued with PVA to the bottom of the roof card, and, almost immediately above this, another strip with similar proportions is glued to cover the gaps above the wall. When I made the Denchworth stable I was not aware of this procedure and cannot have studied the prototype photographs carefully enough, this feature being overlooked, much to the detriment of the model.

Above these two first courses I then hold the sheet of paper and mark on it the vertical cutting lines for the next course, at an acceptable distance from the cuts below. While doing this I insert an extra one or two slates, so as to reduce the size of each one by increasing their number over the same distance, as in *Fig. 70*.

By marking the cutting positions on the sheet, using the previous course of glued-on slates as a guide, there is less chance of the gaps lining up with one another, it can happen though, especially if the model roof is to sag between rafters. To ensure that the unprototypical lining up of gaps does not occur too often, I may cut the strip into

Fig. 70.

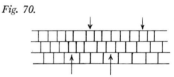

Plate 78a. The limestone slate-covered roof of the Friends Meeting House.

several pieces and adjust their positions along the roof when gluing them in place. A rather large gap can appear at the end of such an adjusted part strip, but I find that preferable to a large number of gaps coinciding.

Periodically, as I work my way up the roof, I check to find out whether I have an acceptable number of slates in the courses compared with a similar position on the prototype. In my opinion a gradual reduction in size is more important than having exactly the correct number on the roof, as correct scale gaps and variations in slate sizes would probably not look sufficiently rustic to be really convincing, even if they were possible to create.

On the roof shown in *Plate 78* the first course was made of a strip including 38 slates, with an average horizontal measurement of 2⅔ mm and an average vertical measurement of 2 mm visible, plus 4 mm overlap area. Twenty-two courses were laid, the top course of which includes 63 slates, with an average size of 1⅓ mm horizontal × 1½ mm showing vertically. The overall dimensions of the roof I have been referring to above are 107 mm × 45 mm.

At the ridge I apply the practice shown in *Fig. 63*, on page 58.

Painting Limestone Slates
As the paper used is very absorbent, the paint for the undercoat has to be very thin though usually well loaded with colour (I know this may seem contradictory but the consistency of paint mixes I use ranges from not much more than tinted water to a fraction thicker than the top of milk). If the paint is not runny enough, the blotting action of the paper draws all the paint from the brush so quickly that blotches result. The undercoat requires flowing brush strokes to achieve a consistently thin application. If, on the other hand, a varying density is required (and when dealing with limestone slates this is quite possible) perhaps for an area that has been attacked by frost, where the very top layers of slates have been flaked away, revealing fairly clean stone, a very pale undercoat indeed will be necessary. In such areas, instead of returning to the palette to reload the brush with colour, I dip the brush into my jam-jar of clean water and quickly brush the water onto the area in question. Inevitably the brush would still have had some colour in it, and some of the paint from the surrounding area is also attracted by capillary action, though not unacceptably so, in fact quite the reverse, as it has the effect of blending the edges of the very pale and not so pale areas (no hard lines or sudden changes).

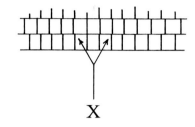

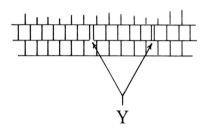

Fig. 71. To avoid tile gaps coinciding, as in X, I cut the strip into shorter pieces and realign, leaving gaps as in Y.

I then paint each slate individually, at random if just a subtle variation is required, or not so randomly if there are noticeably darker or lighter areas. The basic colours I choose are: Raw Umber, Raw Sienna, Chinese White, Charcoal Grey and sometimes a touch of Oxide of Chromium. Again the shades I mix do not necessarily contain all the above (in different proportions) but they may do, depending on the effect required.

On jobs like these I am convinced that a little luck has helped me, and that successful mixes can come without applying very much logic. Experience does help but I have found that things do not automatically turn out better because of it. Complacency can set in and lead to a casual approach that sometimes works but often leads to a less than satisfactory result because a small but vital precaution may not have been taken or an important constituent of a paint mix has been left out. Altering the colours once they have been applied is very difficult and sometimes makes matters worse. If in doubt I try the colours on a scrap piece of paper first.

Plate 78b. When modelling limestone slates, I trim their edges very carefully, before gluing them in place to avoid a mechanical looking finish.

Plate 78c. Limestone slates on the small shed that accompanies Lilac Cottage in the village of Bishopstone.
Roye England

APPENDAGES

Additions to the model after it has been folded into a box.

GUTTERS

For the manufacture of common half-round guttering I have made myself a simple press tool. It consists of a piece of ⅛″ thick aluminium sheet approximately 6″ × 6″ plus a 9″ length of piano wire just over 1 mm in diameter. Using the wire as a cutting tool, I have produced a groove in the aluminium which fits the wire fairly snugly accommodating just over half its diameter, as in *Plate 79a*.

Across the groove I lay a piece of shim metal, somewhere in the region of 2-3 thou in thickness. So far I have used brass and a piece of pure nickel that somehow came my way. Both seem to be suitable, though for some reason I think I prefer the nickel. The material is placed over the groove and the wire gently tapped into it with a small hammer, thus forming the shim to the shape of the groove. The excess shim is then trimmed from either side (Plate 79b).

The positions of the joining sleeve projections and bracket clips, in which the gutter actually rests are determined from photos, and represented by soldering narrow strips of gutter material around what will be the underside, as in *Plate 80*.

To attach the gutter to the wall I have sometimes used small pieces of card glued to the wall plate just under the eaves, but if the support brackets are particularly noticeable then I feel some effort has to be made to represent them. My attempts in this direction have, I am afraid, not been very successful but this is what I have done.

I temporarily glue the gutter (to the appropriate slope) under the eaves and then drill small holes in the wall at suitable positions beneath it, often two courses of brick below. I then push small pieces of bent wire into these holes reaching up to the strips that represent the bracket clips, to which they are carefully soldered. Having fitted all the necessary pieces of bent wire, the whole assembly is then taken from the model (gently breaking the temporary tacks of glue) to be painted.

As I usually work from old black and white prototype photographs, the question of colour has to be resolved. If there is any doubt then I paint the gutters black, but occasionally there is enough evidence to suggest that they should be painted the same colour as the doors, windows, wall plates, barge-boards or whatever. In the latter instance there is often a bit of a problem as the 'whatever' will have

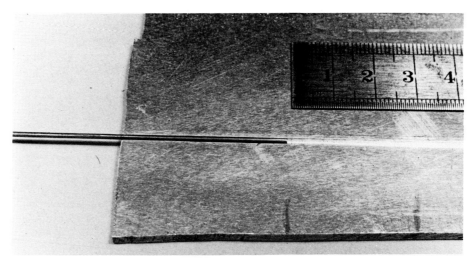

Plate 79a. A groove cut into aluminium sheet in which I form metal shim guttering with the piano wire as a press tool.

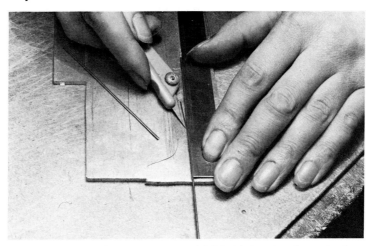

Plate 79b. Trimming the press-formed gutter material. I hold the edge of a steel rule on to the top of the piano wire to keep the shim firmly in the groove. I then trim the unwanted metal away with the 'rough jobs' craft knife, running it along the top surface of the aluminium sheet but actually cutting through the shim against the piano wire. The picture shows a curving sliver of shim that has been trimmed off and to the left is a pressed and trimmed length of guttering ready for the next stage.

Plate 80. In this photograph a pressed and trimmed gutter section has been placed on the piano wire and is secured by soft wire twists. The other pieces of metal are the strips that have been soldered on the gutter to represent the clips and joining sleeves, the ends of which have yet to be cut off. Gutter end stops are made by soldering a small piece of shim material across the end of the gutter and then filing it to shape.

Plate 81. This picture of Willis' Cottage shows the gutter fixed in place under the eaves. I am reasonably happy with my method of gutter production but less so with the support brackets.

Plate 82. A length of copper wire with hopper and joining socket wires soldered on. I would not actually make the pipe of various pieces but from one length of wire bent at the appropriate places with joining socket representations. At junctions another piece of wire would be soldered on, the fillet of solder being filed to shape. As with metal gutters, Humbrol paints are used.

been painted with a special water colour mix which will not adhere to the metal of the gutters very well. If I fail to produce a really good colour match using matt Humbrols then a bit of weathering and rust colour is painted over to disguise the poorly matching colour. The inside of the gutter is painted with either a rust or green algae colour. After painting, the assembly is glued into position using the little pieces of wire and perhaps the odd tack or two between the gutter and the wall plate as well.

GUTTER DOWN PIPES

For these I normally use copper wire of approximately 1 mm diameter, slightly stretched between vice and pliers to straighten it.

To represent the joining sockets, I nowadays wrap two pieces of thin wire around the 1 mm material and solder them, the build-up of solder between and around the thin wires representing the projection of the socket from the pipe. Across what will become the rear, I then solder small pieces of metal strip to represent the ears through which the prototype fixings would go. In the model's case these strips are glued to the wall with impact Evo-Stik.

A hopper of some sort is usually found where the down pipe is not directly connected to the gutter. Whether they have been almost box-like or the more common six-sided, tapering version, I have made them from

Plate 83. In this end view of Willis' Cottage there is a short piece of gutter leading to a rainwater hopper and a drainpipe leading to a water butt.

solid materials, sometimes carved from wood, but more often than not, filed from nickel silver. The latest one, which is now fitted to Willis', had its upper flange and fixing ears made from a strip of nickel silver, bent in the appropriate places, soldered to the top of the filed body. As the strip projected above the body a little, it had the effect of creating a hollow appearance. For the entirely solid ones the hollow effect has been produced by carving or drilling away some of the top of the body.

PORCHES

There now follow three illustrations of porches, the first, *Plate 84*, shows one attached to the Old Vicarage. The two low brick walls were constructed as a small portion of cellar, glued to the main building when the former had been embossed and painted. On top of the walls, two pieces of card were glued to represent stone capping. The roof structure was then made and painted, tiles and all, and glued in place. I then constructed the trestle supports, using card uprights and paper strip for the diagonal crosses. These I painted after they had been fixed in place and the glue had enough time to set sufficiently to accept the water colour without it dissolving too quickly and falling apart.

The two other illustrations show porches built upon platforms at the ground line. In

Plate 84.

the case of *Plate 85* the platform and roof structure were glued on and then the four front uprights fixed between the two. The scribed cardboard infill was then cut to fit between the uprights, and between the corner uprights and the wall, great care being taken at the gluing stage to prevent any overspill. A thin bead of glue was brushed along the edge of the card that would touch the wall; another bead was then brushed along the top of the platform and up the corner posts where the card would touch. Holding the card in tweezers, it was gently pushed against the wall from outside the framework, it was then released from the tweezers which were then used to push the card into place, against the wall side of the corner post. By fixing it in place this way, any over-provision of glue at

Plate 85.

Plate 86. Canney Row. *A. E. Smith*

the corner post would be hidden behind the front boards, although any excess on the painted wall would have to be gently scraped away. When fixing in the front boards, the glue was brushed on to the uprights and platform only, any excess being pushed inwards and out of sight when the card was pushed into place.

Plate 87 shows two porches of very similar construction. For their sides a thin balsa wood frame was made, overlap planked with 0.2 mm pasteboard and then painted. The roof structures were made with card but planked with cartridge paper (as the prototype overlapped edges did not seem as thick as those on the sides) and painted.

With the model laid on its back, resting on a sheet and small blocks of foam, the four main components (platform, sides and roof) were glued in as quick succession as possible to allow any minor adjustments required before setting.

DOOR HOODS

These are often made in the same way as porch roofs but instead of sides they can have a variety of supports, from straight stays to shaped brackets. I have modelled them with a lead covering (writing paper) that can be surprisingly near white in colour, clay tiles, limestone slates and thatch. There are no golden rules — they can be assembled on the bench and then glued to the building or constructed in place and painted *in situ*. Whichever way suits the situation, porches

Plate 87.

Plate 88. Flashing around a chimney on the Leather Bottle's stable.

Plate 89. Cement flashing.

and door hoods are only fixed in place as one of the last few jobs, especially on a building like the Leather Bottle *(Plate 7)* where the projection would have interfered with the laying and trimming of the thatch.

FLASHING

Lead flashing may not be particularly noticeable when modelled well, but it can be conspicuous by its absence. That shown in *Plate 88*, took only 5 minutes for each side of the chimney. I cut a strip of thin paper approximately 3 mm wide and long enough to run the full length of each join to be covered (three separate pieces around the chimney). The strip is folded in half along its longitudinal centre line and lodged in place with friction. Cutting marks, faint pencil lines, are then made on the side against the brickwork to correspond with the mortar grooves, a horizontal line (where the prototype lead is actually folded into the brickwork) and approximately 45° cut-backs to start the next horizontal line below, and so on. When cut out, I brush a little glue to the underside of the folded paper and put it in place. As mentioned earlier, lead often weathers to almost white, so very little paint is required, and I normally use some from one of my slate mixes.

I make cement flashing by using very runny Polyfilla, painted on with a small brush. Two coats are usually needed as the first one often shrinks into a slight trough and numerous little holes appear, but an additional covering (when the first coat has set) normally deals with these shortcomings.

The colour can be the creamy brown of mortar, though usually fairly liberally covered with green algae and various lichens.

CLIMBING PLANTS

In most cases, climbing plants at Pendon have been made using foam of some sort or other, which does not bear close inspection. There are certain notable exceptions, though, like the Virginia Creeper growing up Priory Cottages. This has individual paper leaves made by our railway signal authority, Stuart Johnson, but coloured and glued in place by Roye. Many of the plants in the Chapel Group Garden have also been modelled using paper.

Plate 91. A close-up of some roses to show construction technique. They don't normally look this bad.

For the Russian Vine seen in *Plate 21* I used well teased out Woodland Scenics foliage mat (stuck on with white PVA) and painted it with matt Humbrols, the little flowers being touches of creamy white paint on some of the foam particles.

I made the rather scruffy-looking roses shown in *Plate 91* by gluing Woodland Scenics foam to pieces of bent wire. The flowers are represented by pieces of foam painted with 'rose colour'. At close range, as in the photograph, the construction method is far too

obvious but at 2-3 ft the overall impression is quite acceptable (by my standards).

Plate 92 was taken when I was producing ivy on the end of Willis'. To the right of the model is a block of coarse rubber sponge, from which I broke off small lumps, which in turn were torn into very small pieces, as shown in bottom centre. Holding a tiny piece in

tweezers, I dip it into a blob of glue (the white mess on the tin) and position each particle on the model. Many pieces are required, packed together quite tightly up the centre line of the growth and thinning out at the edges. There are two areas being worked on here, one starting to the left of the water butt, going up the drain pipe, the other starting on the left-

Plate 90. Many people feel I must have great powers of concentration and patience, but mine pale into insignificance by the total dedication given to the modelling of this Virginia Creeper that grows on the front wall at Priory Cottages. This is, of course, the work of Roye England.
A. E. Smith

Plate 92.

hand side of the attached shed and climbing up the edge and spilling onto the roof.

I paint the foam with a mixture of gloss and matt Humbrols, a very dark green deep into the growth, getting paler towards the surface and edges. I cannot produce particles small enough to make up the fingers of new growth at the very ends, so these leaves are painted on the wall.

Although *Plate 93* does not feature any climbing plants, I thought it was worth including to show the weeds growing between the paving stones. These are from the Woodland Scenics scatter materials range (powdered foam) whereas the clumps of grass are made of the wind-catching part of clematis seeds, though not the seed itself.

Plate 93. A small yard at the upper end of Wharf Cottage.

WEATHERING

Plate 94a. Five roofs and not a gutter in sight, thatched roofs seldom have them anyway, but I am surprised that the tiled ones are without them. A good thing from the modelling point of view, for there would be quite enough work just creating the subtle weathered effects, without yards of guttering to make.

Roye England

Having glued on all the various appendages, I take a fresh look at the nearly complete model. Even if I have already copied areas of weathering, I often find they need further attention. Some weathering techniques have already appeared in different guises as part of the descriptions of painting bricks and stones, so parts of the following may seem vaguely familiar.

Practically any surface (except thatch), that may need a feint colour addition, can benefit from a dry brush application of a brownish green or a fairly pale green. For this job I have an old brush that has worn down considerably. With very little water, when the brush is gently rubbed over the surface of the paint in the palette it will, of course, only pick up a small amount of paint. Straight away I gently rub the almost dry brush on a piece of scrap card until very little paint is being transferred. This is the time to use the brush on the wall, rubbing gently over the desired area in a soft circular scrubbing action which leaves the required feint trace of weathering colour on the wall. I use this technique on walls, doors, planks, roofs — in fact almost anywhere that needs a feint dusting of extra colour.

For walls that are in need of re-pointing, the dryish brush is held at a shallow angle so that the weathering colour is only transfered to the surfaces of the bricks or stones, leaving the mortar pale. If, on the other hand, the mortar needs darkening and the 'dry brush' technique does not seem to be having the desired result, I choose a fine line brush (often my brick-painting brush) and very carefully run a very wet and thin mix into the mortar grooves (this cannot be done very well if the grooves have disappeared during the mortar wash or if the grooves were not made deeply enough at the embossing stage). The runny mix, which is sometimes not much more than muddy water, is coaxed along the mortar lines with just the very tip of the brush.

Sometimes I feel that a large area needs mellowing in some way, because some stones or over-painted mortar lines seem to have too well defined or jagged edges, or perhaps a slight overall change in colour is needed. To remedy this appearance I have very carefully floated a particularly thin wash all over the wall, making sure that only a very little of the existing paint is disturbed. This technique is not for those who lack confidence or experience, as the previous painting of the wall can just as easily be ruined as improved. The softening effect it has is very rewarding but beware — it is a very risky operation.

The green algae covering on walls and roofs can range from quite dark to an almost synthetic-looking bright pale green. For the base of the darker mixes I use Oxide of Chromium and then add such colours as Raw Sienna and Raw Umber; at the paler end of the range, Viridian and Aurora Yellow are the main colours. In any event very little Oxide of Chromium is needed as it is a very powerful colour.

For the dirty looking areas sometimes seen at the base of walls (especially if the building has no guttering), I use Burnt Umber, Oxide of Chromium and Charcoal Grey, applied very runny or by the 'dry brush' technique.

For lichens (usually found on roofs) of the 'golden yellow' kind I use Aurora Yellow and Cadmium Orange, whilst for the pale greenish/whiteish/greyish kind I use Chinese White, Viridian, Raw Sienna and Charcoal Grey. The proportions of these colours cannot be conveyed here, but if only a very little of each is added to the mix at a time, then nothing too drastic should happen. Whether little blobs of paint or a light dusting is

Plate 94b. The same range of buildings as seen in Plate 94a. They were connected with a magnificent farm in the tiny village of Knighton, just off the 'Portway' which runs along the southern edge of the 'Vale' at the base of the Berkshire Downs. No free range pigs here, but gates, fences and blocked up entrances to discourage such wanderings. How stark and unnatural the mortar looks compared with the way virtually everything else has mellowed.

Roye England

required of course depends upon the prototype, but if the blotchy type is required it is very easy to have the blotches looking more like regular spots than they should. If the blotches are made up of many small dots they seem to turn out better, but only if the dots are closely spaced. If they turn out looking too solid, I dot them with tiny spots of charcoal grey.

I have often noticed small dots and patches of brown accompanying the lichens on cement flashing and limestone slates, for instance. I know that in some cases the small 'dark chocolate' coloured areas are a sort of dried up moss; Burnt Umber with perhaps a little Charcoal Grey is a suitable mix for this feature.

No texture worth a mention is created with just paint, for the application of a thick mix for the 'golden yellow' lichen, for example, has a tendency to shine, which, of course, is quite unacceptable. I create texture for particularly thick growths of mosses (dried or otherwise) by brushing tiny mounds of runny Polyfilla onto the roof, and, when set, painting them. The first time I used this technique was on the thatch of Breakspeare's Cottage. I was working from old black and white photographs and needed to check on the colour of summertime, non-shaded, thick moss on a thatched roof. I knew of a thatched cottage in a nearby village (near to my home,

not Breakspeare's) and went out one afternoon to see if it had any thick moss on its roof and to my delight it had. I collected a mental colour picture of the moss and quickly returned home to paint the Polyfilla mound that I had made for the moss, just below Breakspeare's chimney. I very soon arrived at what I thought was a splendid colour mix and was well pleased with the result while my attention was focused solely on the mound of moss. However, when I sat back to take in the overall impression, the moss stuck out like a sore thumb and was far too bright. I still think that the colour I had mixed was a very good match to the real moss I had been looking at only an hour earlier, but that was at fairly close range, in real sunshine and, of course, I was looking at the real and unchallengeable world. Looking at a 4 mm scale model 3 ft away (which represents 75 yds or so) in the modelling room or Vale Scene showcase is quite a different matter. I toned down the brightness of the moss and it blended in much better.

My workroom has a mixture of tungsten and fluorescent lighting, to simulate to some extent the conditions inside the Vale Scene showcase at Pendon. But on quite a few occasions I have taken a part finished model to the Museum in what I thought was a satisfactory condition only to find the appearance of the colours changing quite

alarmingly. This change seems particularly noticeable with clay tiled roofs and on one or two occasions it has been necessary to alter the colour dramatically, working at the Museum and checking progress by setting the model in its final position from time to time during the alteration. In one case I washed the roof all over with plain water, taking off quite a large amount of the paint by picking it up on the brush and wiping it off on a tissue. Wash is the correct term, but don't imagine a torrent of water, just a flowing brushful on an area approximately ¾″ in diameter at one time, the use of too much water would probably dissolve the PVA and so the tiles could lift. I did manage to achieve a satisfactory result by completely repainting the roof with a slightly different selection of colours, painted individually on each of the tiles, in different proportions to the original effort; then of course it needed re-weathering. Nowadays I take my models to the Museum for checking at a much earlier stage, but it shows what an enormous effect the type of lighting can have.

That concludes the sequence of operations I usually adopt when making Pendon cottages, though there have been a number of exceptions to the 'normal folded card box' construction, these being described in the following section.

EXCEPTIONS
and materials not already covered

Plate 95a. The Old Vicarage, Steventon. As a matter of interest, I named this model *Il Cimento dell' Armonia e dell' Inventione* after a set of concerti by Antonio Vivaldi. The reason for this may become apparent later.

TIMBER-FRAMED BUILDINGS

For timber-framed buildings, as with buildings of any construction, I study the photographs very carefully and decide where the joins are to be made. If the building appears to be composed of individual parts (additions built against previous additions) it might be preferable to adopt the same components when modelling the building. I also look for any objections against using the normal folded card technique — for instance if the corners and walls seem to bulge and the building has jetties, then folded corners are not really practical. One answer is to have joints at each of the corners and another is to build the timber frame of timber, but I will come to that later.

If the building does not seem to have bulges or other complications I employ the standard box construction. Having decided where to make the joins, I transfer the measurements from the scale drawings to the flat card, allowing the normal 30 mm cellar depth below the datum line. Lightly pencilled outlines of the timbers, window and door apertures are drawn on the card, usually one

elevation at a time. It is my preference to cut out the door and window apertures before scoring the edges of timbers or embossing for brick or stonework.

Many timber-framed buildings, especially those with brick infill, have the brick panels projecting from the timbers, sometimes by over an inch. To create this impression on the model, one can carefully cut through just the surface of the card at each side and end of a single timber, peel away the surface skin and put it to one side, then (with the rough jobs craft knife) gently scrape away the body of the card to the required depth. The peeled away skin strip is then glued back into the trench that has been created and the edges of this broad, shallow trench can be chamfered to take away the hard line.

On buildings where the above mentioned feature is not apparent the outlines of the timbers can simply be scored, being careful not to carry the scoring across the timber to which it is joined. This possibility can be lessened by accurate drawing at the outset. The embossing of brick panels is best done next, obviously avoiding the scoring of

mortar lines into the timbering. The painting of the timbers comes at this stage, for if a little timber colour strays on to an unpainted brick or plaster panel, it can be picked off the plain card with a damp brush. This is not so easy if the panel had been delicately painted with a light plaster colour.

As already mentioned, timber-framed buildings with jetties, bulging walls, and walls that are not at all upright, including panels of infill which are at different angles to one another, may prove impossible to represent adequately by using the standard 'folded box' method. It is possible to cut two pieces of card with matching curves, which, when joined together would make a bulging corner post, but with a joint line down the middle of it. However, not being at all convinced of my ability to adequately disguise such a line, I decided upon an actual timber frame for the front and sides of the Old Vicarage model. The separate infill and timbers, facilitate the representation of panels at varying angles.

For those who think that this method of construction is more appropriate for their chosen prototype, I have endeavoured to

Plate 95b. The rear of the Old Vicarage where the timbers are part of the wall card, their edges being defined by scored lines. (The top of the chimney has yet to be finished.)

convey the technique, using the sequence of events in modelling the Old Vicarage as an example. The individual processes of construction of the walls can, I feel, be of assistance in modelling any similar prototype.

I tackled the structure in three separate sections, left wing, centre portion and right wing. This placed the joins to be disguised at either end of the central section, at both the front and back, the front ones being at 'inside corners' and the back ones conveniently beside vertical timbers rising from the ground line to the eaves. For no special reason I started with the right wing section, for which a piece of card was marked out to include the four cellar walls and enough card above the datum line for the brick and stonework below the sill beam on which the timber was to be erected. The brickwork of this very low wall was, as usual, completed to the all but weathered state before the card was folded and glued into a box around a pre-checked floor.

The timber for the frame had to be absorbent but not coarse grained, as twelve inches to the foot grain would not look at all convincing. Most balsa wood I have come across has suited very well.

The first timbers required were the sill beams, so measurements for these were taken from the scale drawing. The visible thickness of the timber was, of course, the most important dimension, unless the end of a timber protruded from the wall, in which case the width also mattered. The best material I found was sheet balsa of a suitable thickness so that little trimming or sanding was necessary.

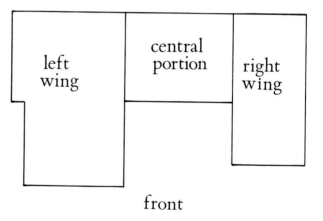

Fig. 72. *A plan of the Old Vicarage, showing its three main components, which could initially be modelled separately and later joined together.*

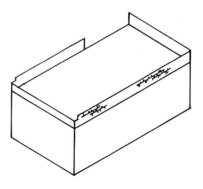

Fig. 73. *A folded box cellar and low brick wall on which to build the timber frame.*

I cut a strip, along the grain, keeping the knife hard against a straight edge, to prevent straying with the blade. The strip is cut to length by laying it against a steel rule on a cutting board, using the knife as a stop to align the ends. The knife is then positioned along the strip at the desired measurement taking care that neither rule nor strip move. When the blade is lightly pressed in position on the strip, the rule is moved out of the way and the second and third fingers of my left hand are then placed on either side of the blade while making the cut, as in *Plate 96*.

After the sill beams had been glued in place, the corner posts were the next timbers to be tackled. The order of construction of the jetty on the front elevation of the right wing required careful consideration. The main posts for the lower storey were carved to shape and notches cut at their tops to accept the wall plate of the lower storey. Having placed a smallish spot of glue on both the sill beam and bottom end of a main post, the latter was held in position for thirty seconds or so. Both surfaces were glued, especially the end grain of the main post, because in some cases the balsa seems to absorb the glue like a wick.

Both these main posts had to lean back by approximately 1 mm at the top. With the model on a sheet of glass, a six inch square was placed in line with the bottom of the post and the top was then gently prodded to the correct distance from the square before the glue had hardened. The wall plate at the top of the lower storey was then glued into the notches at the top of the main posts, as in *Fig. 74*.

Plate 96. Cutting strip balsa to length. By doing the job this way, it is possible to cut the timber without either end of the strip flying away, thus saving much time that might otherwise be spent searching the bench and floor for a stray piece.

Resting on the joints of the wall plate and main post, were timbers that ran along the side elevation walls at more or less first floor joist height, supported at opposite ends by upright timbers. The front upper storey main post and appropriate upright timbers at the ends of the side wall plates were then erected, as in *Fig. 75*.

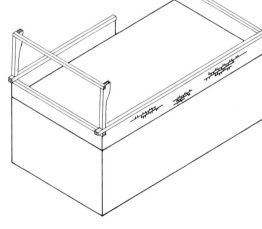

Fig. 74. The beginning of the timber frame for the right wing portion of the Old Vicarage.

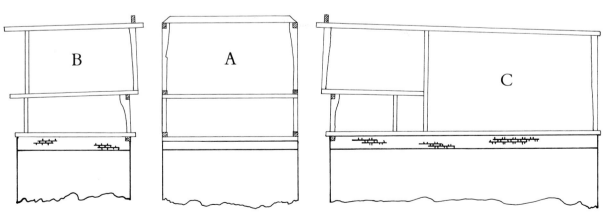

Fig. 75. A later stage in timbering the right wing. (A) Front elevation. (B) Left-hand side elevation. (C) Right-hand side elevation.

With the main corner posts and wall plates assembled, the gable and intermediate timbers were then fitted, (this time obtaining the lengths for the latter from the model rather than the scale drawings) checking each one in place before gluing.

This flimsy and easily damageable timber frame was then braced temporarily at its most vulnerable points with strips of spruce (stronger than balsa) as in *Plate 97a*.

The card for the brick panels had horizontal mortar lines scored on it before cutting each shape from it. The fitting of the panels turned out to be quite a time-consuming job, as each one was initially cut with a little to spare on all sides, and then trimmed to an acceptable fit. The vertical embossing of the brick panels was done back on the bench after the fitting check had been made because the brick bond could only be ascertained when the exact shape and size of the panel was known.

Each panel had to be a gentle push fit, as final fitting with glue on the edges was far too likely to result in some of the glue straying on to the visible surfaces of the timbers and panels. To avoid this, each panel was wedged within its surrounding timbers and a fillet of glue was brushed around the inside perimeter.

Plate 97a. Looking inside the right wing portion with timbers erected, panels of card fitted and painted and the temporary spruce bracing.
A. E. Smith

Plate 97b. As this method of construction had not previously been used at the Museum, the right-hand wing was advanced beyond the rest of the model so that it could be offered to Roye and the rest of the buildings team for approval before going any further — the contest of harmony and invention — hence my name for this model.
A. E. Smith

The window frame of the right wing, upper storey window, which had its frame virtually flush with the structural timbers, was made from a piece of card, cut and fitted like a solid panel, and then marked and cut out to leave the central upright. Glazing bars were then glued across the back of the frame, as described elsewhere. This delicate frame and glazing bar assembly was next positioned correctly within the structual timbers and lightly glued from behind. When the glue was hard the assembly was painted, and then glazed with acetate sheet. This was fitted within the surrounding timbers, behind the window frame, and an inner frame, made up of separate card strips, was positioned behind the glazing and glued to the structural timbers to hold the glazing material in place. This seems easier than actually gluing the glazing, bearing in mind all the adverse possibilities when working in such a confined area.

As the walls were erected upon a pre-folded cellar, the majority of them could not be painted as a flat sheet of card. Therefore, to facilitate the painting of the part built model, it was laid on its sides on a clean piece of thin foam and a sufficient stack of flat tins and boxes to the same height as the walls was placed in front of it to rest my hand on. The

Plate 98. A tranquil scene taken at the Old Vicarage, Steventon, in the 1920s, we think. Normally the timbers of such buildings, in the 'Vale' area, did not receive any preservative treatment although it appears here that something very dark has been applied, as they are usually a very silver-grey colour. When I measured the building for modelling in the 1980s there was still quite a trace of old tar on the timbers. *Pendon Museum*

Plate 99. Close-up of the right-hand side of the right wing portion showing panels of plaster and brick with only a hint of whitewash left.

timbers were painted with a thin and very pale shade of 'timber colour'. I knew I could make them darker at a later stage if desired, but not easily paler. This covering of the balsa was sufficient to create a general impression although when the plaster panels were painted with an off-white wash and the brick ones completed in the usual way, the timbers did appear much too pale. However, by applying several coats, each using a fractionally darker colour, a satisfactory overall impression was soon achieved.

For even darker areas, where the prototype had traces of tar or pitch, I gently stroked a much dryer mix on to the specific timbers, but as with other buildings, any further weathering would come when the model was more advanced. From this stage onwards the procedure was much the same as for a conventional model that had been folded into a box.

Plate 100a. The left-hand end and rear of the left wing section. The rear timbers scored in the wall card, the end and front more or less made in the prototypical manner, a self-supporting framework of timbers.   *A. E. Smith*

Plate 100b. A front view of the three sections, in different stages of completion. They were not joined together until later.   *A. E. Smith*

Plate 101. A quite large timber-clad barn from Denchworth.

TIMBER-FRAMED AND TIMBER CLAD

Farm buildings such as barns and byres were very often built with timber frames clad with weather boarding. Even for a building of this construction I start with a cellar floor cut to the correct ground plan and marked with the positions of the various posts. Gaps are cut to accept these before the cellar walls are folded and glued around the floor and, when the cellar has been completed, the corner posts are erected. These are rebated (to accommodate the thickness of the card) at their bottom ends before being pushed through the holes provided, and glued to the inside surface of the cellar walls. The wall plates are glued on top of these, sagging and curving as necessary, and then the main and intermediate posts are cut to fit, and glued under the wall plates — this is much easier than trying to fit a wall plate to a whole line of posts that had probably been cut either too long or too short. Any tie beams that may run across such buildings are glued to the wall plate above the main posts, and then any posts that may support the tie beams are glued in place. At this stage the floor is covered with a not too runny Polyfilla mix (to represent the usual earth floor) and then painted to the finished condition.

The structure is now ready for the weather boards which are cut from 0.2 mm card. Often 5 mm wide strips are used, divided into the visible and overlap areas, approximately 3½″ and 1½″ respectively (for waney elm the planks are often quite a lot deeper and, because of the waves in their edges, a larger overlap area is called for). Starting at the base of the wall, the first boards are glued in place, at a similar angle to those that will be glued above them, brushing some glue on to the top edge of the cellar and an adequate spot on to the posts, at the appropriate height. Subsequent boards are secured by brushing a thin line of glue onto the previously laid board, right at the very top of its outer face, which will be covered by the next board to be fitted.

One elevation is completed at a time, working upwards and around any door and window apertures.

As the insides of the walls are often visible in such buildings, it pays to be very careful not to allow glue to stray onto the inside surfaces that are to be painted. If glue does stray onto visible surfaces it can be scraped away quickly and the area washed over with a pale, 'inside' or 'outside', timber colour mix (I keep the brushes, palettes and water handy during construction). When the building has been completely planked, I paint the inside as it is much easier to work around two or three tie beams rather than a whole host of roof support timbers, not that I model all of them. The colours I use for inside are Raw Umber, Raw Sienna, Chinese White and Charcoal Grey.

As the buildings of this style I have so far modelled for Pendon have not been destined for positions where the visitors would be able to see up into the roof, I must admit to some corner cutting as far as roof framing has been concerned. To me the roof starts where the principal rafters join the tie beams above the main posts. These rafters, with or without purlins, are usually glued in place along with a collar supported by queen posts, with another vertical post rising from the centre of the collar to support the ridge beam, as in *Plate 103*.

The remaining roof timbers are simply painted on the under-side of the roof card and may include purlins, common rafters, tile battens or laths. The roof timbers that I do

Plate 102.

Roye England

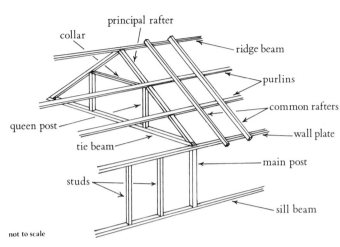

Plate 103. Looking inside Willis' Barn/Shed. This shows the amount of roof timbering I normally model.

Fig. 76. Names given to various structural timbers.

Plate 104a. The severe twist in the roof of Willis' Barn meant that the roof card needed holding in place for quite a time while the glue set. I was not prepared to sit and hold it there!

Plate 104b. The roof card glued in place. Unfortunately, the photograph does not show the twist.

Plate 105. A small implement shed across the road from the Leather Bottle. A hole was cut in the roof card, and rafters and laths made of balsa and card were glued in place behind it.   *A. E. Smith*

Plate 106. What a delight this picture is for those who appreciate corrugated iron, not that I really come into that bracket. It is Badbury Farm, after nearly all the thatch had gone, although there is still a little to be seen on the farm house roof just above the hipped end of the right-hand barn. Perhaps Roye does not actually detest corrugated iron but he certainly does not appreciate it in large amounts and would only model it if he had to. *Roye England*

model are painted before the roofcard is glued in place. The roof of Willis' barn had quite a severe twist that needed copying, and a very makeshift set of temporary retaining apparatus came into play while the glue was setting, as can be seen in *Plate 104a*.

CORRUGATED IRON ROOFS

I have had to represent corrugated iron roofs on quite a number of models, some on buildings that seem to have been built with the material, others where the original roof covering has been replaced by corrugated iron, and even some where the odd sheet or two has been pushed into thatch to cover a particularly leaky spot. In all these cases the corrugations have been at 3 inch centres, although I believe there was a 4 inch centred material used before the turn of the century.

I have always used rolled metal sheet; the old Slater's copper was a bit over scale, but acceptable nonetheless if the model was to stand no closer than say 2 ft from the normal viewing position. I heard of some American rolled aluminium intended for the 3½ mm brigade and thought that if it was manufactured to the same accuracy as the British equivalent it should be pretty near for my 4 mm requirements. However, I was wrong,

Plate 107. Willis' Barn with its roof of corrugated iron, painted to represent the early stages of rust setting in.

Plate 108. The Pendon corrugated iron rolling mill, made by Stewart Hine.

and found to my disappointment that it is manufactured to a considerably higher standard and is as spot-on 3½ mm as makes no difference. Although under scale for us, I think Campbell's corrugated iron (available from Victors of Islington) is acceptable for really close viewing conditions.

Of course it is possible that true scale material viewed from over 5 ft would look too flat, but then that is well over a scale 100 yds away, so perhaps it should. However, the theory and practice of scale perspective is a very difficult subject to resolve to everybody's satisfaction, so, in the main I try to keep to scale whenever possible. My efforts may not result in true scale representation every time and there may in some cases be an advantage in a little exaggeration of some texture or other, but I would have set out to make it accurately and the exaggeration would be the result of failing to do so. The amount of exaggeration that is acceptable is of course in the eye of the beholder. However, that's enough philosophy!

On the vast majority of models I have used brass and aluminium sheet with corrugations created by passing strips of sheet through the mill shown above.

On occasions I have even cut the strips into scale-sized sheets and used them in the correct positions on the model, but the overlaps are very difficult to make neatly enough to be very realistic. I now favour long strips, preferably the full length of the building, and at each of the appropriate positions I scribe a line with a sharp point to represent the vertical joins. In most of the photographs I have worked from, vertical overlaps have been nowhere as near as noticeable as the horizontal ones, and therefore I now only model the latter.

Cutting the strip to size is not quite as straightforward as it sounds, especially across the corrugations; scissors squash them somewhat and they have to be reshaped to allow a neat and tidy overlap, either horizontally or vertically. When cutting a long strip, (either as a continuous line or as a series of staggered ones) I use a steel rule and the 'rough jobs' craft knife. This method results in a little burr, part filling each trough end, but this can be

remedied using a small round file. If the corrugations have been flattened a little I use a metal scriber (the diameter of which is compatible with the radius of the corrugations) to reshape them. With the job on the bench I run the scriber along each trough, going out and back a few times to restore the distorted ends.

Having cut a strip to size, both it and the area on the roof card to which it will be fixed are coated fairly generously with Evo-Stik Impact Adhesive and then brought together in the prescribed manner. I find strong impact adhesive essential as the rolling inevitably puts unwanted stresses into the material which can have a tendency to twist in some way, usually in the opposite direction to any such twist that might be desired, because of the shape of the roof.

During a conversation on the subject of corrugated iron with Nick Britton, a multi disciplinary modeller for Pendon, he was wondering if overlaps could be made more satisfactorily if paper were used somehow. I thought about it afterwards, not least because it would enable me to paint the roof with artists water colours, and came up with the idea of laminated aluminium sheet with paper.

The following procedure is, I think, only possible if one has access to a rolling mill. A strip of aluminium was cut to fit the mill and then evenly coated on one side with 3M Spray Mount. After a few seconds the strip was pressed onto a strip of 30 gram air Conqueror paper approximately 2 mm larger (on all sides) than the strip of aluminium. While the Spray Mount bond between aluminium and

Plate 109. Willis' Barn, one strip of rolled aluminium glued in place and the upper one (in front of the model) waiting its turn.

Plate 110. A laminate of thin sheet aluminium and paper halfway through the process of being corrugated in the rolling mill built by Stewart Hine.

paper was still fresh the laminate was wound through the mill, as in *Plate 110*.

The projecting paper is trimmed back as necessary to give the required amount of overlap, or overhang at the eaves, with the obvious advantage of a more delicate appearance. However, when trimming, the paper corrugations are unavoidably distorted and some attention is even more necessary, in restoring the shape of the corrugations. This can be done using the metal scriber, by rubbing the paper into a spare piece of corrugated metal, in the case of the eaves or into and over the lower glued-on strip, in the case of a horizontal overlap.

Some corrugated iron roofs completely rust away in quite large areas. To produce this effect I carried out a small experiment in etching.

The piece of corrugated copper shown in *Plate 112* was painted on both sides with cellulose grey primer, and small areas of paint were then scraped away from both sides to reveal bare copper. A Pyrex saucer with about 5 mm of ferric chloride was then heated over an inverted bench lamp. When I thought the liquid was warm enough, the corrugated copper was gently slid into the saucer to avoid splashing any of the potent acid.

For the next 20 minutes or so I gently stirred the ferric chloride and pushed the piece of copper about with a matchstick to disturb the very dark substance that formed on the areas being etched. This is apparently made up of broken down copper and ineffec-

Plate 111. The rear of Willis' Barn covered with laminated and rolled aluminium/paper. The copper wire on the ridge is used as a foundation for the paper ridge capping.

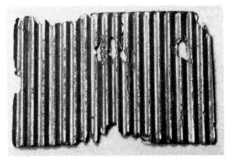

Plate 112. A scrap piece of corrugated copper that I used when experimenting with the possibility of representing rusted away areas by etching.

tual etchant, and, if much of the dark substance was allowed to form, the etchant in the saucer could not do its work, hence the continual stirring, prodding and general agitation of the job.

When sufficient material had been etched away, the sample was taken from the ferric chloride and placed in a saucer of plain water by hooking a piece of wire through one of the etched holes. The lamp was then turned off and, when cool enough to be handled safely, the contaminated etchant was flushed down the loo and the saucer and etched copper washed thoroughly.

Plate 113. Not a very cottage-like building I admit (a Great Western weighbridge office to be exact) but the construction principles apply to cottage outbuildings.

Plate 114a. A small lean-to structure at the rear of Canney Row. The water butt was made from Slater's copper rolled around a pencil and then soldered together. Note the imperfections at the eaves of the right-hand portion, squashed and unrestored edges that are also far too wavy compared with the left-hand portion. I think the material was half hard brass (not very suitable).

Plate 114b. Corrugated iron with the beginnings of rust showing. As can be seen in Plate 106, the horizontal overlaps are far more important features to represent than the verticals.

CORRUGATED WALLS

On a few occasions I have had to make small buildings with walls as well as roofs of corrugated iron. For these I make a card box, incorporating any doors and windows and clad it with the rolled metal. Because the corrugated iron has to be worked around such features, the use of long strips is virtually ruled out, and good overlaps are essential. The corners can be a bit tricky as they often come very near to the sheet's edge. I make sure that the very edge that will form the overlap around the corner, is straight and then with the sheet lightly clamped in the vice, I fold the predetermined amount (projecting above the jaws) by pushing with a steel rule held just above the fold line.

PAINTING CORRUGATED IRON

When painting the paper/metal laminated material, the Artists Water Colours I use are as follows: for a fairly new galvanized finish, Charcoal Grey, Chinese White and just a touch of Raw Sienna. The same mix is used, but to different proportions, for a weathered tar or bitumastic finish, but for an all over 'old rust' effect the main colours are Burnt Sienna, Charcoal Grey and Burnt Umber. For the more orange looking 'newish rust' I use Cadmium Scarlet, Cadmium Orange and Burnt Sienna.

When painting on just the rolled metal I use Matt Humbrol Enamels: Light grey, black, red oxide, white, and dark and light earth, though not necessarily all of them mixed together at one time. As with Artists Water Colours, if just black and white are mixed together, a very bluish grey is normally the result (not a very common colour) and to overcome this problem I add a touch of light earth colour which has the same effect as Raw Sienna water colour.

STONEWALLS WITH A PRONOUNCED TEXTURE
and Wattle & Daub

From time to time I have had to model walls with quite noticeably textured surfaces, for which the normal embossed card technique would not produce a sufficient amount of relief.

The example shown in *Plate 116* was created using Polyfilla which was carved, when dry. This technique was also used to create a couple of such features at one end of Willis' (what a useful model for illustrations it has been), as seen in *Plate 122*. Apart from decayed chalkstone, two panels of wattle and daub needed representing (with the wattles

Plate 115. The garden wall here is a prime example of the sort of stonework that I would create using the Polyfilla (carved when set) technique, though not for the buildings, as they appear to have much flatter surfaces. I wonder what the brick and stone lean-to on the main building was, with what seems to be a glass-fronted notice board — post office, police station or maybe something to do with a bus company? *Roye England*

Plate 116. The upper end of Canney Row where the cement rendering has fallen away to reveal coarse stonework.

Plate 117. The white area within the irregular edged brickwork is a sheet of card glued behind the wall and recessed by approximately ½mm. The same applies to the area between the card-made wall timbers above and to the left.

Plate 119. The paper panel shapes, with glued-on cotton, now fixed in place between the timbers in the recessed area provided.

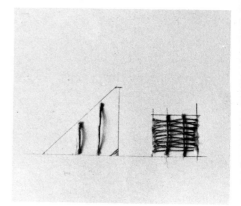

Plate 118. This is a sheet of paper with the outlines of the panels marked on it. The two vertical members, in the left-hand area, are lengths of cotton (glued at their ends) representing oak staves. In addition to similar verticals, the right-hand area has woven horizontal cotton threads, glued in place to represent the wattles (either hazel or cleft oak).

showing) on the same end of the cottage; so I will describe the two jobs together, since they were modelled as a combined task.

As can be seen in *Plates 12 & 18*, I removed areas of the wall card where the stonework and wattled panels had to be. Before the painted walls were folded into a box, I glued a piece of card to the inside surfaces of the walls, across the cut-away areas to form a backing, onto which I could build up the plaster stonework and wattled panels. The model was then folded and glued into a box, as in *Plate 117*.

As the panels with wattles showing were to receive some Polyfilla, the representation of the wattles was tackled next, so that the whole job could then be plastered in one operation.

I next mixed the plaster for the stonework and daub: a runny mix of Polyfilla, water and a little Resin W (PVA), not too much of the latter as when the time comes for carving, the mix could have set with a consistency not unlike granite (not very easy to carve).

With the model standing on end, so that the plastering could be done with the wall horizontal, I gently brushed the runny mix up to the edges of the brickwork and timbers, and then filled the areas in the middle, so the plaster projected a little from the wall. Two coats were necessary to fill in the little holes that appeared.

At one end of Mill Cottage the irregular stonework was not at all well defined and had been limewashed, so carving was thought to be unsuitable. Instead a technique devised by Penny Thompson was used; small screwed-up pieces of Kleenex tissue were glued, side by side, on the bare card wall and when dry, the wall was covered with runny Polyfilla. When

Plate 120. The Polyfilla mix brushed into place, now set and awaiting carving.

Plate 121. A close-up of the wall, showing plastered wattles and the now set Polyfilla mix, having been carved ready for painting. For the carving I use a scriber and sharp pointed file and scratch away at the surface until I reach the desired depth.

approximately two-thirds of the way towards setting, I rubbed a plain water-loaded brush over the surface, to create the lumpy though smooth appearance (more plaster in between the pieces of tissue than on them). Brushing with water also seems to reduce the possibility of a smooth skin forming.

PAINTING PLASTER CREATED SURFACES

As the plaster is very absorbent and draws the paint from the brush very quickly, a wet mix is used so that hard edges are not left between areas of one application and another (returning to the palette for more paint and then back to the model). A side effect of this is that the plaster changes colour with the damp, it also takes longer to dry than card, so the immediate appearance of colours cannot be judged until dry. As with many other jobs, only a little colour is applied at a time. It is possible to take off some of the colour (if too dark for instance) though never completely. Carved mortar lines/grooves or gaps between stones can be painted in the same way as with card, also the 'dry brush' weathering technique works just as well when used on plaster.

Plate 122. The finished model, painted and ready to be set into the scenery.

Plate 123. The almost undefinable irregular stonework on one end of Mill Cottage, modelled using tissue and plaster.   *A. E. Smith*

Roye England

COLOUR APPENDIX

The following colours are all from Winsor & Newton's 'Selected List' Artists Water Colours. The ingredients listed under each category cannot be taken as anything more than a guide, proportions of colours must be arrived at by trial and error, and reference to the text on pages mentioned may provide some help. For thatch and metal items the reader is referred back to the main text.

TIMBERS (Tarred, creosoted and weathered)
Charcoal Grey, Burnt Umber and Chinese White; obviously more Charcoal Grey than the others for newly tarred. Likewise Burnt Umber for creosoted, and an almost silver grey mix for well weathered timbers. See page 20.

MORTAR (Lime)
Raw Sienna, Chinese White and Charcoal Grey — not much of the latter. See page 20.

BRICKS (Red)
Light Red, Burnt Sienna, Burnt Umber, Cadmium Orange, Cadmium Scarlet and Brown Madder (Alizarin). See page 21.

BRICKS (Blue)
Payne's Gray, Chinese White, Prussian Blue and Brown Madder. See page 21.

BRICKS (Yellow)
Chinese White, Aurora Yellow, Raw Umber and Oxide of Chromium. See page 23.

OLD WHITEWASH
Chinese White, Raw Sienna, Charcoal Grey and Oxide of Chromium — very little of the last three are needed. See page 23.

LIMESTONE
Chinese White, Raw Sienna, Raw Umber and Charcoal Grey. See page 23.

DOORS, WINDOWS, etc.
Usually dull colours: Burnt Umber with Charcoal Grey, perhaps. Oxide of Chromium with Charcoal Grey maybe. Window frames usually Chinese White. See page 27.

THATCH
See pages 55 and 56.

TILES (Red Clay)
Much the same as Bricks (Red). See page 61.

TILES (Asbestos)
Light Red, Brown Madder, Chinese White and Charcoal Grey. See page 62.

SLATES (Welsh Type)
Davy's Gray, Brown Madder, Viridian and Chinese White. See pages 64 and 65.

CORRUGATED IRON
See page 86.

A BRIEF SUMMARY OF THE SEQUENCE OF CONSTRUCTION
I USUALLY ADOPT

Field Work — Page 1

Measurements, noted on sketches of the building, and photographs from as many angles as possible (including views taken at right-angles i.e. 'square on' when possible) along with notes of colours and any peculiarities there may be, are essential for the making of a satisfactory model.

Scale Drawings — Page 3

From information on the dimensioned sketches and the photographs, scale elevations and plans are drawn. Some modellers work straight from their surveys, but a scale drawing offers an appreciation of the building and its proportions in scale size, which is not only very useful during the modelling procedure, but can help to avoid mistakes. Dimensional anomalies often show up on the drawing before any commitment to construction.

Joins and Folds — Page 9

At this stage decide where on the model the inevitable joins and folds are to be made. Some buildings have convenient changes of materials where joins can be made, others have lean-to additions behind which joins can be hidden. Whatever the case, careful thought given to these decisions will pay dividends.

Laying out the Card — Page 10

The type of card used is important for reasons of texture and longevity. The pencil lines marked on the card must be feint and few.

Apertures for Doors and Windows — Page 12

Cut out these apertures before any further work is undertaken. This task may seem a simple one, but some very undesirable effects can be created if great care is not taken when using a craft knife.

Embossing the Card — Page 16

Very often in one wall, stones, bricks and timbers are mixed together. These need separate consideration. Having identified these areas by lightly pencilled outlines on the card, it is time to represent their differing appearances, usually by embossing the surface of the card. Depressions in the card to represent mortar lines between bricks and stones and around timbers leave the stones, etc. in relief.

Painting — Page 20

I prefer to do the majority of the painting when the card is still in the flat as it is easier to control the brush, although some weathering, and often the painting of roofs, is done when the model has been folded into its eventual shape. The painting of individual bricks and stones can take a very long time but if everything goes well, it can be very enjoyable and satisfying.

Preparing the Card for Folds and Trimming to Shape — Page 25

The card now comes off the drawing board. The removal of some card from behind the corner lines is carried out now in preparation for the folds that will come later. The trimming of any unwanted card from around the walls is carried out at this stage as the card is still of a single thickness.

Illuminated Rooms — Page 26

Not everyone will want to illuminate or even fully detail an interior but if this is to be done the choice of which rooms to furnish and illuminate dictates which doors and windows should be modelled open. The concealment of the light source also has to be considered before decisions regarding the floor plan are made.

Doors and Windows — Page 27

Having decided which doors and windows should be modelled open, the various layers that make them up are cut from thin card and painted, before they are glued together and fixed to the walls.

Folding into a Box — Page 33

It is desirable to have a floor ready cut, around which the walls can be folded. This floor may have to include holes for the distribution of light to the rooms.

Interiors — Page 35

I make the funished rooms detachable during construction — they are sealed in for good when the ceilings are glued in place.

Internal Strengthening — Page 38

The rooms that are unfurnished do not remain empty but provide an opportunity to add bracing for strengthening to prevent the walls bowing in or unduly bulging.

Chimney and Roof Card — Page 40

Chimneys that appear in the slope of a roof or at the ridge are best completed and glued to the internal strengthening before fixing the card on which the roof covering is to be glued.

Roof Coverings — Page 43

The task of covering a roof, especially with tiles, can be a most laborious operation. Slates, on the other hand, are larger and consequently not quite as bad, and thatch, perhaps surprisingly, is appreciably easier still.

Appendages — Page 67

By this I mean features that are not integral with the folded box. These include porches, door hoods, gutters, climbing plants, etc.

Final Weathering — Page 73

Although some weathering may be done while the card is still on the drawing board, the majority is done when the model is virtually complete. The overall impression is better appreciated, and the various parts of the building can be blended together to better effect.